Confidence!

Confidence!

Justin Phillips

HODDER AND STOUGHTON
LONDON SYDNEY AUCKLAND

Copyright © 1994 by Justin Phillips

First published in Great Britain 1994.

The right of Justin Phillips to be identified as the Author of the Work has been asserted by him in accordance with the Copyright, Designs and Patents Act 1988.

10 9 8 7 6 5 4 3 2 1

All rights reserved. No part of this publication may be reproduced, stored in a retrieval system, or transmitted, in any form or by any means without the prior written permission of the publisher, nor be otherwise circulated in any form of binding or cover other than that in which it is published and without a similar condition being imposed on the subsequent purchaser.

Unless otherwise indicated, Scripture references are from the HOLY BIBLE, NEW INTERNATIONAL VERSION, copyright © 1973, 1978, 1984, by the International Bible Society. Used by permission.

British Library Cataloguing in Publication Data.

Phillips, Justin
Confidence!
I. Title
158.1

ISBN 0 340 59208 7

Typeset by Hewer Text Composition Services, Edinburgh
Printed and bound in Great Britain by Cox & Wyman Ltd, Reading.

Hodder and Stoughton Ltd
A Division of Hodder Headline PLC
338 Euston Road
London NW1 3BH

To Laura, Rhiannon, Isabelle and Bryony

CONTENTS

Preface ix

1 Confidence in question 1
2 Confidence at work 25
3 The confident colleague 47
4 Resources for confidence 63
5 Confidence in the future 95
6 The confidence eaters 127
7 Confidence in Christian origins 155
8 Confidence where it counts 185

Recommended reading 211

PREFACE

We were sitting in a hotel restaurant in Washington a week before President Clinton's Inauguration, waiting for the black coffee to go with our breakfast. We were there to broadcast a special edition of *The World Tonight*. As I was about to tuck into my bacon and hash browns, I couldn't help but notice this lady of, shall we say, generous proportions, who came in and sat down at the table next to us. She ordered steak and eggs for breakfast. A plate arrived so packed with food that it landed with a thump on her table. The steak seemed to sit up and beg for mercy. The eggs were resigned to their fate. As she began to devour her steak with all the relish of a carnivore, she picked up her breakfast reading. It was a book called *Essentials of High Self-Esteem*.

All of us to one degree or another struggle with self-confidence. To some people confidence seems to come naturally until they face some unexpected setback. For others, it is a lifelong struggle to like themselves and discover a sense of self-esteem. For the Christian, the assurance that God loves us as we are is a great liberation, but it does not necessarily solve the confidence issue quickly or easily. Confidence can be very tricky indeed. This book argues that confidence comes from within and can be built up with work and prayer and some planning. None of us is content with the idea of just muddling along through life. We all want to make the most of our lives and to find fulfilment and satisfaction. If we are to be positive and confident in ourselves and in our future, if we are able to let God develop us to be more Christ-like in our character and approach, then we will see the benefit.

This book aims to get beneath the surface to give us a new

confidence in who we are, in where we are going and in what we believe. We begin with a look at the confidence gap and our struggles with confidence, not least my own. We then tackle specifically how to be more confident at our place of work with a survival course on some of those difficult situations that can trip us up – from avoidable blunders to resolving conflict, personality clashes and coping with setbacks. We explore the resources for confidence available to us, both physical and spiritual. The chapter on confidence in the future handles questions on how we use our time and how we can plan ahead, with some exercises to help us set priorities.

The second half of the book takes on those areas that undermine Christian confidence – misunderstandings over science and faith, and issues such as suffering and disasters. We take a new look at the origins of Christianity, its history and archaeology, and rediscover how solid the ground is on which we stand. This book urges us to take our lives in our hands and to go forward with God. The basis is a blend of biblical principles and practical application, liberally sprinkled with stories from my own life and experience. I should point out that some of the illustrations and anecdotes are of such a sensitive nature, that where appropriate I have changed names and identities to protect the privacy of those whose stories I tell. All biblical references, unless otherwise indicated, come from the New International Version.

The idea for this book came out of a number of conversations with friends and with my publisher James Catford. I would like to thank James for his gentle encouragement and assistance with the manuscript. Others have helped me at various stages with ideas, suggestions and criticisms. Roy Castle, Robert Court and Sandy Wickenden read relevant parts of the manuscript and made helpful contributions.

Deepest thanks go to my wife Gill, who has had to live with this book as well as me since its inception. Her encouragement, comments and patience have been a rock to me. My children Laura, Rhiannon, Isabelle and Bryony have given me much inspiration and released me on Saturday mornings to write. I am indebted to other friends for their help and stories, especially those at my local church, Haven Green

Preface

Baptist, among them Phil Belsham and Keith and Cag Wilson. Special thanks go to David and Lillias Chawner, our minister and his wife, whose teaching and friendship have contributed so much.

This is my own work and the views expressed in it are mine and mine alone and do not in any way purport to represent those of the BBC, my employer. I am grateful to my personnel officer, Lesley Behrendt, for permission to write this book, which was done entirely in my own time. It is my hope and prayer that every reader will not only derive pleasure and enjoyment from it, but will emerge at the end of the journey we share together more confident as a person and in faith. Nothing would delight me more.

Justin Phillips

1
CONFIDENCE IN QUESTION

'Justin, you're a sensible fellow, how can you believe all that religious crap?' So began a not untypical exchange at work about my faith. This was a bright, talented journalist asking me how I could possibly believe what he considered to be garbage. The question was put in a forceful but not unfriendly way. This was a double challenge – both to me and to my faith. I could either take the easy way out, smile and ignore him, or I could stand up and be counted. He was questioning not only my confidence in what I believed but also my willingness to stand up to him. I decided to reply with a frankness to match his own: 'Because I believe it's true and it works and if you take a decent look at the historical evidence you'll see why'. Although as a journalist he was prepared to approach most things with an open mind, on matters of religion his thinking was like reinforced concrete.

For him, all religion is a fairy tale and has no place in the real world. Christianity is a relic of history and has nothing to offer. How strange that someone like me should openly defend it: it made no sense at all – to him. He tried to put me right. 'Jesus probably didn't even exist,' he went on. In this kind of banter, there can be no real meeting of minds or dialogue. This was a verbal jousting match in which we charged past each other on our horses with little hope of the lance striking home. There was no animosity, but to him I remain misguided just as to me he remains lost in the maze of his own ignorance.

In a situation like this, we may feel that we are being questioned at two levels. First we are being asked about our convictions. Are we prepared to defend them? Are we confident in what we believe? Secondly we may well feel that our personal confidence is being questioned. Are we prepared to stand up and be counted, in this case as a Christian? Our personal confidence is put to the test, that quality of trust and assurance we all have to one degree or another. Confidence gives us the boldness to take the opportunity to respond. One of the most confident characters amongst the first Christians was Peter, the fisherman-turned-disciple. In his first letter to the churches he urges his readers '"Do not be frightened." But in your hearts set apart Christ as Lord. Always be prepared to give an answer to everyone who asks you to give the reason for the hope that you have' (1 Pet. 3: 14–15). Confidence is that ability to be sure-footed and strong within ourselves in the good times and the bad, when life is running sweetly and when we seem to be up against the odds.

THE CONFIDENCE GAP

Nick is thirty years old and is an accountant – a good job in a big-name firm. He had been praying consciously for an opportunity to talk about his faith to a colleague. He had been trained in his local church on how to share his faith and is not the kind of Christian to shy away from a chance to talk about it. Yet the fact of the matter was, that one day he was completely taken aback by the most simple of questions. A colleague at work asked him, 'What is a Christian?' Nick corpsed. His head knew what he wanted to say but there was some indefinable block – fear perhaps, embarrassment or plain shock. Whatever it was, Nick found he could not give a straight answer. He fumbled for words and his colleague changed the subject. The opportunity had gone past faster than a hedgehog can roll into a ball. There was a confidence gap.

Despite all the assurances any Christian believer could hope to find in the Bible or hear from the pulpit, the fact is that many Christians find themselves struggling to live a normal Christian life in the rapid-change high-tech society in which we live. In conversations with friends and colleagues and family members we find ourselves caught short. We can't find the answers to questions they pose, or we just don't know what to say. Instead of being ourselves we start to rely on techniques or jargon, which invariably let us down if they do not match our natural personality.

It is little wonder that the confidence of Christians in our faith and in our churches has taken a battering in recent years. Quite apart from our own shortcomings when it comes to sharing our faith, we find that we are having to start from a very low level of common knowledge about Christianity. The level of understanding of what we believe and why is so much lower today than it was for our parents' generation. I am constantly taken aback by how little people know about the Christian faith. I really shouldn't be, as it has been well documented in surveys. A MORI poll (the *Daily Mail*, August 4th, 1992) found that 57 per cent of eighteen- to twenty-four-year-olds could not say what happened on Good Friday and 62 per cent did not know who Pontius Pilate was.

A Gallup survey for *The Times* to discover how much influence religious belief has on secular Britain today produced still more gloom. In this case the sample of 600 interviews with students, teachers and professionals was chosen specifically to produce a 'best possible scenario'. The outcome was depressing. Asked to quote any verse from the Bible other than from the Lord's Prayer, 50 per cent of those interviewed and 73 per cent of students were unable to do so. Out of eleven religious writers including the likes of Bunyan, Milton, T.S. Eliot and C.S. Lewis, 23 per cent could not name a single religious work by a single writer. For only one writer (Bunyan) could more than half name a work. For the researcher, 'the dominant impression left was of a society that has not so much rejected the Church as one that knows little about it'.

There is no getting away from it: Christians have a communication problem. We can no longer assume that people are familiar with the basic beliefs of the Christian. They are not. Hardly a week seems to pass without another book coming out that claims to put the final nail into the Christian coffin. Few of these arguments are new. People either claim that Jesus did not live, or did not die, or did not rise, or is not who we Christians claim he is.

Frankly, however clever or persuasive these arguments first appear, they usually fall apart under closer examination. Two thousand years of Christian history and experience are not going to be demolished by any number of such books. None the less, they can leave an imprint, eroding the confidence of some and seeming to chip away at the edifice. They can add to a feeling that Christians are either kidding themselves, or are several sandwiches short of a hamper. It's a bit like Chinese water torture – it's not the drip of water that hurts, but the impact of all the drips continually over a period of time. Christian confidence can become unstuck by the seemingly endless barrage of those attacking Christian fundamentals of faith.

OUR IMAGE DOESN'T HELP

You don't have to look very far to see the popular image that Christians have in the eyes of some, and let's face it, it doesn't help the Christian cause very much. A Christian is all too easy to caricature. Christians are often portrayed in drama as being naive, misguided souls on the margin of society's cutting edge (the dotty vicar syndrome), or busybodies. Christians are sometimes seen as too sincere by half, harbouring prejudices and supporting views which many in society reject as old-fashioned or plain wrong. Worst of all, that's often how some of us who are Christians feel about ourselves: we feel out of touch with our world, or on the margin of our society. Sad though it is to say it, many of us find it a struggle to be open about our faith. We feel marginalised in our place of work and are only too happy to withdraw to the sage and sometimes over-cosy fellowship of our local church groups.

Confidence is often at a low ebb in our churches too. As Christians we may feel unsure about ourselves and our place in the world. Many of our faith's certainties have taken a battering in the years after the Second World War, so that even our confidence in what we believe has become shaky.

Many of our number are unsure that the beliefs we hold most dear are really true. It is as if there has been a steady erosion of our Christian coastline by the powerful secular waves breaking up a shingle foreshore. For so long it has withstood the power of the tide, but the tide has turned and the Christian heritage is now crumbling.

There has been a subtle undermining of confidence over many years for many reasons which we shall explore in the course of this book. I am convinced (he says confidently!) that confidence is generated from within a person. It is not something that can be acquired like a driving licence or put on like a raincoat; neither is it a quality that we can generate quickly or easily. But there is a lot we can do to build up our own personal confidence with God's help. For a start, it is useful if we can develop a slightly tougher skin and be less sensitive about how others see us.

LIVING WITH OTHERS' IMPRESSIONS

A senior BBC figure, who recently left the Corporation (taking early retirement), told me to my face that I was in his words a 'decent and moderate' man. It was intended as a compliment and I took it as such. At the same time I must admit that, at the back of my mind, I wondered if it was a compliment with a slightly barbed edge to it. After all, the phrase 'decent and moderate' can be just another way of saying 'dull and boring'. My esteemed former colleague is not the sort of person to think ill of anyone and I am sure he was paying me a sincere compliment. But it is true that many Christians who lead straightforward lives, drinking moderately, faithful to their married partner, conscientious at work, seldom if ever swearing, moderate in language, lifestyle and behaviour, do run the risk of being seen by others as pious, boring and opinionated! This is not a bad thing at all, it is simply how it is.

In the television drama *Rumpole of the Bailey* John Mortimer has created in the wily old barrister Horace Rumpole a wonderfully crumpled character, generous in spirit. In comparison, Rumpole's Head of Chambers, Mr Ballard, is a dry old stick. He is portrayed as an archetypal Christian – a dull teetotaller, a prudish, mean-spirited man with no sense of humour, who wears his faith on his lapel in the form of the fish badge. Though it grates, there are, I am sure, many Christians just like that in the world of work, uncomfortable with themselves and out of place.

Our social culture does not make it easy for us Christians to be confident and outgoing about our faith. In polite company, religion and politics are often considered off limits as conversation topics. Many people are openly embarrassed when a friend starts to talk about deeply held personal beliefs. There is still a feeling that a person's religion is a private matter for one's own conscience.

Christians who are perceived as high achievers in their work often have a greater freedom to express their faith than others. The newspapers and magazines are full of examples. You would have to have spent the last decade on the planet Mars not to know that Cliff Richard is a Christian, or to be unaware of the difference that his deep personal faith made to entertainer Roy Castle in his struggle with lung cancer. In the world of sport, there are many examples. When American tennis player André Agassi won Wimbledon in 1992, most newspaper profiles of him described him as a Christian. Colourless and dull Agassi most certainly is not. Controversy is part of his public appeal and often clouds his apparent Christian credentials. There are many Christians on the tennis circuit. Michael Chang usually makes time to take part in the tennis service at All Souls Church, Langham Place in London during the Wimbledon tournament.

The popular British athlete Kriss Akabusi is very open about his faith. During the Olympic Games in Barcelona Akabusi wrote in the *Radio Times*: 'I've always been a confident person. I was a success in the children's home, when half the kids went to jail. In the army, I was a sergeant at 22. Success has followed me round every corner. I have faith in my ability'. Akabusi continues, 'I've only been a Christian for five years, but in my whole life I can see the hand of God. Each day, I spend an hour praying and reading the Bible. I'm very aware that my talent has been given to me by God and I constantly thank him for the successes and for the failures that I can learn from'.

Now that is the confident expression of a man who knows himself and has a sense of direction in his life! Because he is seen to be a success, winning a gold medal in the World Championships relay in Tokyo and two bronze medals in the Barcelona Olympics, his Christian statement is acceptable. Yet for those of us who can't run around an athletics track in twenty minutes, let alone forty-eight seconds, our faith is not always as well received. We may well encounter real hostility.

CRACKING THE PROBLEM

Most of us don't have the exuberance or confidence to let our faith bubble out like Kriss Akabusi or Cliff Richard. Faced with our friends we feel more like the dormouse in *Alice in Wonderland* – wanting to hide in the teapot – than like the outgoing Queen of Hearts. Our faith is a bit like the Cheshire Cat: we appear with a smile on our face but happily fade away into the background when put on the spot about where we stand.

If we are rebuild our personal Christian confidence, we must be prepared to take some personal measures. None of us is satisfied by feeding off the faith of others – like a hyena waiting for a lioness to abandon the prey when she has had her fill. All of us want to be confident within ourselves. So let us resolve to tackle the roots of self-doubt within us and to lay down new roots of trust in God. This may mean some painful decisions. So how can we begin the process of renewing our personal confidence? Are we prepared to brace ourselves to take a look at who we are? It is not easy to be honest about ourselves and there are times when we are bound to think to ourselves: whoops, I've done it again!

It is a fact of human nature that, whatever standards we set for ourselves, we will fall short. Interestingly, when Paul talks about sin in his letter to the church in Rome, he uses the language of archery. 'All have sinned and fall short of the glory of God' (Rom. 3: 23). The verb used for 'fall short' can also be used to describe an arrow failing to reach its target from an archer's bow. Paul goes on to say right away that all who are Christian believers through their faith in Christ have the perfect counterweight to the failings of their natures. Though we fall short of God's glory we are put right or 'justified freely by his grace through the redemption that came by Christ Jesus' (Rom. 3: 24). So this is the backdrop.

It is Jesus who puts right our relationship with God. Getting to grips with ourselves is something we can achieve only with some honest self-appraisal. We may find that there is still a lot of doubt in our minds about what we believe as well as about who we are. So let's have a go at hacking away at the weeds of doubt about what we believe. We can then set about reassuring ourselves that our faith is based on real historical facts, not hearsay from the past.

There is an English proverb, 'Confidence is a plant of slow growth'. How do we set about growing our own confidence? No one who lacks confidence can become confident overnight. This book is not attempting to turn introverts into extroverts, or vice versa. It is not a manual of techniques to enable you to put on a more convincing mask than the one you wear already, or to polish a veneer that is beginning to fade. What we hope to do is to deepen and strengthen your personal confidence, both as an individual and as a Christian living in today's sometimes hostile environment.

LEARNING TO BE OURSELVES

There is a delicious saying that 'you are what you eat'. On that basis, some of us are bowls of muesli, others are double cheeseburgers! What we want to be is authentically and uniquely ourselves. If the recipe is right for you, then your Christian flavour will be strong and wholesome and will come through. It is possible to be comfortable with who we are, with what we are really like. Being at ease with ourselves is not beyond any of us. It may take a long time and a long struggle to achieve, or it may just as easily turn out to be a relatively gentle process. Whether we are quiet or noisy, shy or extrovert, tall or short, is irrelevant. Confidence is a reflection of who we are. Isaiah the prophet put it like this: 'In confidence shall be your strength' (Isa. 30: 15 AV).

If Christians are to take centre stage and not be squeezed into a secular mould that may bear little resemblance to reality, we no longer have to be a wimp for Jesus. Something can be done about the roots of self-doubt. In order to gain more self-confidence, it is essential to have a clearer grasp of who we are. This may mean facing up to the areas of our life where we do not feel as strong or effective as we might like. We will find we are taking a look at our weaknesses as much as our strengths, our failings alongside our successes.

Let me use a simple illustration to explain the importance of recognising who we are in reality and of coming to terms with that, instead of trying to become someone we are not. It is the story of Cuthbert. Now Cuthbert has been a member of our family household for about seven years now. He is bright yellow with a distinctive fringe. That's right: Cuthbert is a canary. He was bred for captivity and has already lived a long and healthy life by canary standards. He doesn't sing as beautifully as in his youth, but nowadays he's a gentle bird in his dotage. If we were to pretend that he was a wild bird and set him free, he would be lucky to survive an hour. A bright yellow songbird would be far too conspicuous in a garden habitat where most birds are brown or black. If the magpies or robins did not go for him, one of our neighbourhood cats would quickly see him as an easy target. To release Cuthbert into the wild would be cruel. He is what he is – a bird bred for captivity to sing. In that role he enjoys a long, safe and, we hope, contented life.

I tell that story to make the point that in the process of becoming more confident, it's helpful if we start where we are with who we are. Let's not pretend at any point to be someone other than ourselves. We are working towards building up our confidence as we are, not as someone we are not.

So let's begin by doing some honest self-assessment of our strengths and weaknesses, our qualities and our talents, those areas of our life that are under control and those that are not. There is no substitute for a long, hard look in the mirror of our life from time to time to see a true reflection of who we are. This book will help you to take control of your life; to take away those obstacles that get in the way of what God is wanting to do. It aims to remove the traffic in the avenues of your life that are slowing down your personal growth and development. It is underpinned by the belief that God wants us to be fulfilled and whole as individuals and free to be truly ourselves and to be truly available for him to shine his light through us.

If we are going to start to get to grips with who we are and what we are really like, it is only fair that I should tell you something about myself, so that we can make this journey of Christian self-discovery together. The goal of our trip is first to build up our confidence in ourselves, as individuals, hand in hand with God. Let's do this in a spirit of adventure, opening ourselves to whatever surprises God may have in store for us along the way. It's a bit like watching the London Marathon. Each athlete has twenty-six miles to cover, whether man or woman, able-bodied or disabled. Along the route the organisers give out drinks and refreshments to sustain the athletes on the journey. What a welcome surprise a cool drink must be to a hot and sweaty runner. So let's prepare ourselves for what we may discover on our route to Christian confidence, ready to be handed a refreshing surprise just around the corner.

MY CONFIDENCE STRUGGLES

Confidence is an issue I had to face from a young age. I was born prematurely and was small in size. I spent the first days of my life in a maternity hospital fighting for life. It was two weeks before I was five pounds in weight. Only very recently did my mother reveal to me that I nearly died in my infancy in her arms. On one occasion I had a convulsion, stopped breathing and was turning blue when in desperation she instinctively put me to the breast to get me to breathe again.

With two older sisters and an older brother, it wasn't easy to hold my own in a large, growing family. I never felt short of love but as the youngest of four, I felt I had to compete for attention. I can still remember standing in my cot looking anxiously out of the window when my father came home with a new car. All the others rushed outside to see it while I was restricted to standing in my cot, leaning over the bars to peep through the curtains. It must be one of my earliest memories. I felt excluded from some great family event. I was jealous and angry and no doubt burst into tears, which is how we cope with these crises when we are under five years old. Just because I was a mere toddler and had gone to bed, everyone assumed wrongly that I was asleep. I not only felt I was missing out, but out of the window I could see that I was. It seemed to be the price of being the youngest. Then everything changed with the birth of my third sister.

When I was five years old, along came my little sister Fenella. We all adored her; she was the apple of our eyes. My brother was then eleven years old and my two older sisters were fourteen and seventeen. Now I was a middle child – never easy. Suddenly to see a small sister whom I loved so much become the focus of all the family's affection and attention, as it seemed to me then, was strange and unsettling. I felt I had lost my footing and was confused. My pleasure at gaining a pretty little sister was tempered by feelings of envy. These feelings passed but I remained rather tense and highly strung as a child and seemed to feel things deeply. I remember sensing real fear at seeing thunder and lightning for the first time in a storm over the sea, when we stayed at a seaside holiday cottage. Life was so big and I was so small. The security of the family around me gave me some confidence, but it was not my own; it was a feeling of love and protection coming from them.

THE TRAVAILS OF CHILDHOOD

I was the sort of boy who would get so excited by a birthday trip to the circus, that I would be sick as soon as we got there. The prospect of seeing Coco the Clown and the animals performing their tricks was more than I could bear. My stomach knotted up in excitement with the inevitable result. All children feel vulnerable and sensitive and I was no exception. My saving grace, so far as my school teacher was concerned, was that she thought I was bright and that made a big difference.

My form teacher thought I had potential that would never be developed properly because of my quietness and the limitations of that particular school. Breaking every rule in the book, the teacher concerned contacted my parents and recommended they send me to a different school! My parents followed her advice. Unfortunately, she wrote such a glowing testimonial to the headmaster of my next school, that he was convinced he was about to receive Albert Einstein at the very least. If only! I felt unable to live up to everyone's expectations of me.

To make matters worse, the Head had put me into a class of older boys, believing that this budding 'genius' would thrive on the greater intellectual challenge. I was very unhappy there. The truth was that I was a perfectly normal boy, bright but not exceptionally so, and now I was getting out of my depth. It was decided to put me down a year into the class below. As you can imagine, my self-confidence at this stage had more holes in it than a Swiss cheese.

To add insult to injury, I also found myself getting into situations I could not handle. One particular teacher we had was struggling with class discipline and on one occasion it broke down altogether. As he entered the classroom, he was peppered with elastic bands catapulted across the room at him. There was fearful retribution from the Head. This was the era of corporal punishment. Every boy in the class with an elastic band on his person was singled out to receive a beating. I had one wrapped around a pack of playing cards in my pocket. A thick leather strap was used to beat the palm of the hand. I was only eight years old. I tried to be brave, but the sting and the shame were horrific. I was very upset. The injustice of it, coupled with the pain and trying to explain to my mother why I had been subject to corporal punishment, was just awful. I felt desperately wronged and unhappy for quite a while after that.

PHYSICAL CONFIDENCE STRUGGLES

What I lacked in physical power in the playground at school I had to make up for in cunning and survivor instinct. Although my wife never quite understands this, I still think of myself as a shy person. By the time I was ten years old my brother was sixteen and my youngest sister was only five. I felt a bit isolated at home, with my brother into teenage interests and my sister barely starting at school. My passions were watching cricket and exploring the universe with my telescope. I was small for my age and wafer-thin and my mother was worried I would be an easy target for any school bullies, so she sent me to boxing classes, to teach me some self-defence and to put some aggression and confidence into me.

There were several school gangs and I decided that the best way to keep out of trouble in the playground was to have a gang of my own. I enlisted a lad whose surname, appropriately, was Hardman to act as my 'bodyguard'. His size matched his name: he was six foot three! School is a great survival course and, for the Christian, one of the toughest environments of all. Children can be very cruel and at that age, it is not smart to believe in God. Religion is for rubbishing. Christians are to be pitied. At this age, many a fragile and unconfident faith has been broken – but, thanks be to God, not mine.

Physically, I felt like an under-achiever. Although I loved sport, I was still smaller than other boys. I could run fast and remember getting to the sprint races in the school sports. Against boys far taller, however, my very best was not good enough to win. In soccer, I found myself playing in defence and likely to come off the worst in a tackle. I did quite well at cricket, but was always on the edge of the school team as a ten year old, never quite in it. Swimming classes were just a catastrophe. During one lesson, I was suspended in the water by a rope tied through a pulley in the ceiling of the local swimming bath. Unfortunately, the rope slipped out of the hands of the instructor and I sank like a stone beneath the water. I thought I was going to drown. It seemed like minutes before I was rescued. By then I was petrified and to this day when I go into the water I tense up and in my mind's eye sometimes relive the nightmare.

Isn't it strange how childhood memories can seem so vivid even thirty years later? It's as if it happened yesterday. I am still in touch with those feelings of my childhood, both good and bad, and all of us to some extent carry with us into adulthood the marks of our youth. Sometimes they are moments of pure joy. Sometimes there are scars and hurts. Trying to remember those moments can be a bittersweet experience, but I am sure that it can be a tremendous help in our search for our true selves and the sources of our confidence or lack of confidence.

For me as a skinny young teenager, the combination of being enthusiastic about sport but failing to get into any school teams did not help my confidence. It was dispiriting to try so hard but to feel that, whatever I did, I was never going to be good enough to make an impact in competitive sport. The swimming incident, too, had really knocked my confidence sideways.

Inevitably, there were still many situations in which I felt uneasy and shy. As confidence develops, it begins to surface in different ways, but often slowly and unexpectedly. Put into a public situation, asked to lead a group discussion or to do a public reading, we suddenly discover within ourselves that we can do it and we are not mortified by fear. We also learn to rely on God, asking him to steady our nerves and let us give of our best.

The pattern continued into my teenage years. I still loved sport, but was never quite big enough or good enough to get into the school teams. At one time, I played rugby three times a week in the wing forward position, now called 'flanker'. For this you need to be fast and tough. My job was to 'kill' the opposite side's scrum half. I could certainly get to him fast, but it was never easy bringing to the ground a boy who was bigger and more powerful than I was. With the knocks, however, you do become tougher and more determined. Every failure made me more determined. In life as in sport, I found that each setback would cast me back on God, more determined to work my way through whatever problem then troubled me. So what appeared at first to undermine my confidence I found could eventually increase it. I found that each setback and disappointment built within me a steely core of determination to face up to my fears and to bring them to God. Confronting them helped me to work through them and to draw on God's strength to come to my weakness. This means that we can change over time as God works with us.

There is no need to give up or to surrender to despair when we seem to let ourselves down again and again. At the heart of the Christian gospel is the good news that God's love for us has no limit, even to the extent of sending his own Son Jesus to suffer and die in our place the death we deserve for the way we live. God's forgiveness to those who turn to him in what the Bible calls repentance and faith is certain and secure. So let's not give up hope. God can and does change us over time.

I found that this principle of trying to turn setbacks into growth points applied in the school classroom as well. I began to get a more accurate sense of what I was good at and the subjects in which I struggled. Slowly I began to trust my own judgment more. The school had labelled me as a budding scientist, so imagine what I went through as exams drew closer and I felt more and more uncomfortable with subjects such as Physics, Chemistry and Maths. My exams were a disaster. I was so disappointed – I got the passes but scraped through with miserable grades. This time it was my intellectual confidence that was being undermined. It took a lot of persuasion to convince my teachers and my parents that I should be concentrating on arts subjects such as History and English and should steer well clear of the sciences. I had been typecast in the wrong role and I had to change direction. When I finally settled into subjects where I was comfortable, everything began to slot into place. My confidence grew and my results improved dramatically. I had discovered something new about myself: that although I am a slow starter, I am a strong finisher. Educationalists today would describe me as a 'late developer'.

I am not a naturally aggressive person and asserting myself does not come easily to me. I have a friend who is painfully shy in a person-to-person conversation. She goes bright red with embarrassment at any compliment. She seems so self-aware that you wonder how she can cope in her job, yet she is able to overcome that shyness and heads up a department of a big national organisation. I am perfectly happy to melt into the background and watch what is going on, only to find myself drawn into some impassioned conversation on some topic or other and having to argue a case in which I may not necessarily have any particular views. I don't like conflict or getting into long arguments and will usually try to negotiate a path through the jungle.

I was always rather good at the board game 'Diplomacy' for that reason, which mimics the state of the world at the turn of the last century. Instead of taking on the world with my armies – part of the game's strategy – I would make deals and build alliances and try to secure victory in the game the long, hard route. I have never had the ruthless streak that double-crosses allies and wipes opponents off the board. I prefer conciliation to conflict and this can be frustrating to the person who is looking for a good row. I have lost count of the number of occasions on which I have been told by colleagues at various times earlier in my career that I am too nice to get far. It gives me great satisfaction to prove these people wrong. Why should I try to be something I am not and compromise my integrity? To be yourself requires a measure of self-confidence.

THE SOAPDISH APPROACH

A friend of mine called John had a confidence problem with people. He decided that he had to do something about his appearance. He went out to spend money on the latest fashions and tried to improve his appearance. He certainly looked different, but to be quite honest, it didn't make any difference to his personal confidence. The problem was in his mind and personality, not his dress sense.

I have argued earlier that confidence comes from within. It's not something that can be bolted on from the outside. A few years ago there was an advertising campaign for a particular brand of toothpaste. The claim was that if we used this brand, the whiteness of our teeth would give us a 'ring of confidence'. Isn't it extraordinary how many advertisements concentrate on what we do when we wash. I call it the soapdish approach. My friend John fell for it. It's as if all our problems could disappear if we used a particular soap or brushed our teeth with a certain brand of toothpaste. In the real world washing in the bathroom in the mornings is a fairly hurried affair. Switch on the radio, turn on the shower or put the basin plug in, turn on the taps, grab the soap and slap it on. Somehow I seem to have missed out on this experience of washing as an ecstatic metaphysical experience better than sex!

If you believe the commercials, the important question is not how clean the soap makes your face, but whether or not the brand is gentle on your skin. The point is this: if we all took the same care to be as gentle to ourselves as to our skin, would we see ourselves in a new light? In other words, if we took half as much trouble about our 'inner person' as we do about our outward appearance, then we would find ourselves in much better order. The words of Jesus to the religious leaders of his day come echoing back to us with all the power of an alarm clock at five o'clock in the morning. Accusing them of hypocrisy – a familiar charge to the religious – he says, 'You clean the outside of the cup and dish, but inside they are full of greed and self-indulgence. Blind Pharisee! First clean the inside of the cup and dish, and then the outside also will be clean' (Matt. 23: 25–26).

The meaning is quite clear. The soapdish approach to life will leave us relying on words and actions – externals – to mirror Jesus Christ to those around us. But what Jesus wants of his followers is to address not the outside but the inside of our lives, the question of who we are. That requires a different approach. The basic ingredients for this process are honesty, humility and an openness to what God wants to do in our lives. Self-awareness is essential to personal growth and development to Christian and non-Christian alike.

A person's true character may not be immediately evident – another weakness of the soapdish approach. How easy it is to misjudge other people and to underestimate them. Appearances can be deceptive. Take my friend John. When I first met him it was obvious that he was artistic. He had a great sense of colour and personal style. It was clear from the way he dressed, the way his room was decorated and in his range of interests. He also had great physical presence: he was the kind of person you first notice when you walk into a room. But it was several years before I discovered that this tall and striking friend was also a worrier. Had I looked more closely I might have spotted that he bit one of his nails and had difficulty holding my gaze, avoiding eye contact. He looked distracted. To my surprise, as I got to know him better, I discovered that John was also a terrific organiser and had real talent at drawing, designing publicity posters for all and sundry. Within his personality, there is a whole community of different Johns. It has taken years to get to know him well.

LOOKING AT YOURSELF

When did you last give your self-esteem a massage? Self-esteem is a measure of how much you believe in yourself, your level of self-confidence. For some people this can go up and down like a yo-yo. For others there is a consistent pattern and an awareness of what is possible and what is not. Each of us has a sense of what the limits are.

Julie is a tall and outwardly confident person. Her height makes her stand out in a room. She is affable, witty and always seems relaxed. In her professional career in finance, she was perfectly comfortable dealing on a one-to-one basis with clients, but put Julie in a social situation with glass in hand and fifty people in a room apparently enjoying themselves and she felt very uncomfortable. In fact the social side to her job in the end forced her out of finance into another career altogether. Despite many personal qualities and apparent confidence, she shies way from groups and is very reluctant to go to any parties. In contrast to Julie, I also know the 'party animal' who is the life and soul with an audience to hear the well-told stories, but is quite lost in an intimate one-to-one setting.

So let's not kid ourselves. There is no gain in pretending or in putting on a brave face. To grow in confidence, we may find that when we ask ourselves how much confidence we have, we may well end up looking at a rather straggly little plant. It may well need quite a bit of careful nurturing and feeding if that plant of confidence is to grow and to thicken out into something more robust. It's rather like the old picture of the acorn and the oak tree. Out of that small seed in its little cup comes the magnificent oak tree which can live for hundreds of years.

Whether we feel our confidence is like an acorn or a young sapling, or is already a tree of some girth, let's examine what we have in our credit account in our personality bank. We'll do this by posing a question. You may at this stage find it useful to have some paper and a pencil at hand to jot down your answers. Here's the question: If you were trying to introduce a stranger to someone who is just like you, how would you describe yourself? What are your good points – those aspects of your personality that you have developed and where you feel comfortable with yourself? I can't abide phrases like 'the feel-good factor', but that is what I am getting at. What aspects of your life and yourself do you feel good about? Let's try to get into a positive frame of mind and start the process of moving forward with a bit more confidence.

WHO ARE YOU?

As we start to ask some more serious questions, think again about your finer qualities. If I or anyone else were to meet you for the first time, say at midday tomorrow, what would I like about you? What would I relate to? When you start to think more positively about yourself, your sense of who you are will grow. It is a curious thing to say, but it is possible to be a stranger to yourself. The human personality is highly complex and has many sides and aspects, like Rubik's cube. As we get to know ourselves better, so our confidence and self-esteem will grow.

We cannot claim the high ground without securing the lower ground first. Mountaineer Chris Bonington could not have conquered Everest without first establishing his base camp, his supply route and the equipment he needed to do the job. Having a sense of self-belief and self-worth is the base camp. The Christian believes that every person has an infinite personal value. That is at the heart of the Christian gospel: that God places such value on each of us that Jesus came into the world to do the business required to put each of us on a proper footing with God. The 'business' was Jesus's own death – more on that later in the book. I ask the question again: How do you feel about yourself? What is your level of self-esteem? Do you walk into a room full of strangers feeling at peace with yourself and sensing God's peace within you? Or are you more like a bar of flaky chocolate, falling apart at the edges and beginning to melt? To become a confident person, you need to know yourself and to feel at ease with yourself.

If that is hard, try to think of some of the things said to you that have lifted your spirits. Think of some of your recent achievements. What has gone well for you and how did you feel afterwards? Think about your qualities as a person. What different sides are there to your character? All these different qualities you have, your interests, your characteristics, the things you like about yourself – think of them for a moment as a family, as a community. It may be useful at this point to write them down.

THE INTERNAL COMMUNITY

Who are the members of your 'internal community' that make up you? Maybe you are artistic or scientific, an organiser or an administrator. Think of your creative skills and the qualities that your friends appreciate. Maybe it is your tact or your kindness, your thoughtfulness and sensitivity, your sense of humour or your good nature. Think why you would like to spend some time with yourself and get to know yourself better. This is not an exercise in introspection but the start of some honest self-appraisal.

You may find you surprise yourself. The minister of my local church, David, is a very good example of how you can learn new things about yourself by putting yourself into new situations. When we had difficulty casting the role of Peter in a powerful musical drama to be performed over Easter, he reluctantly stepped into the role. It was his first time on stage as a performer, outside the pulpit! Yet his performance was one of the most memorable of all – powerful, convincing and moving. He could identify with the part he was playing, but he also put a lot of himself into it and discovered more about himself. It is often when we least expect it and take on something that stretches us, that we find we grow as a person. When a gardener cuts back the old raspberry canes, the new canes that emerge come up from the inside of the plant and are green and strong.

All of this will help us to build up confidence in ourselves and also in our faith. We are on the road to discovering what God wants to do in our lives. Not for nothing has he placed us in the here and now. There are tasks ahead for which God wants to use our special talents. Confidence is a key that can help to unlock the future, by the grace of God. Later in this book, in chapter five, we will look specifically at how we can build up our confidence in the future. That chapter contains a number of exercises to help us think about the future, both in terms of who we are and what our life direction should be, on the firm foundation of biblical principles.

TITANIC CHOICES

To get hold of that confidence key a level of honesty is required that many Christians do not find easy. I recently led a series of Bible-based talks in our local church on Paul's second letter to the church in Corinth. It is a letter that often gets overlooked by churches, maybe because Paul is so disarmingly honest in it about his personal strengths and weaknesses. 'We have this treasure in jars of clay,' he says, 'to show that this all-surpassing power is from God and not from us' (2 Cor. 4: 7).

Paul is not afraid of death and has been close to it many times. His confidence rests in having come to terms with his weaknesses and in his knowledge of what is to come. Three times Paul asked God to remove some unidentified ailment or weakness that tormented him. He called it a 'thorn in my flesh' (2 Cor. 12: 7). But God did not answer that prayer – rather Paul's irritant, probably an old injury or wound from the physical punishment his body had taken over the years, became an asset. He found God's grace to be sufficient and his power made complete in Paul's weakness (12: 9).

Paul goes on to plead with the Christians in Corinth to look hard at their own lives. He calls them to examine themselves, to test themselves to see they are truly in the faith and not led astray by a phoney faith or bogus teaching. Test yourselves, says Paul.

We cannot become a confident and sure-footed Christian without knowing ourselves. That can be a painful process. We may not like what we discover about ourselves. The more fearful side of our character or the darker side of our make-up can be a bit scary, but being a Christian is all about letting light shine into the dark corners and letting God loosen the knots that tie us up and cut the threads that hold us back. If we don't make the attempt, then we are deluding ourselves.

In a moment we'll make a start by plunging into the demanding and challenging environment of the workplace. In our attempt to see how we can cope better in our work and get to grips with the dynamics of organisations, we will see how our confidence can be built up. Sometimes it is a matter of just seeing what is going on around us, applying simple principles and keeping our noses to the ground. Other situations can prove to be tougher to unravel so we'll look at those as well. From confidence in the workplace we'll move on to look at resources we can call upon to increase our confidence. These include such basic necessities for physical and spiritual survival as prayer, quiet and sleep. We then move back to personal confidence with some practical exercises to help us face the future. In chapter six we look at what eats away at Christian confidence before taking a fresh look at Christian origins – can we trust the evidence of history and archaeology? The last chapter draws the threads together and encourages each of us to move ahead in confidence and with God.

All along the way, we will face choices. We can be realistic and look at the reality of our personal landscape, or we can turn a blind eye and pretend that all is well. Like the violinists on the *Titanic*, we can carry on as if nothing is happening around us if we choose, but is that bravery or foolhardiness? Had we been on the *Titanic* in the orchestra, as that great ocean liner struck the iceberg and began to sink, would we have carried on playing our violins, ignoring the reality of our situation, or would we have rushed to the lifeboat? I know what my choice would have been.

2
CONFIDENCE AT WORK

Attempting to be a confident Christian should carry a health warning, but maintaining your Christian values and integrity at work can be especially hazardous. Ask Rebecca. She found herself in a situation which first became awkward, then difficult, then utterly impossible. It ended up in an industrial tribunal.

Rebecca's story received national attention in August 1992, when she won a case against her employer for constructive dismissal. *The Times* ran the story on its front page under the headline, '£8,000 victory for Christian who wouldn't lie' (August 14th, 1992). The *Daily Telegraph* put the story at the top of their Home News page. Their headline was very similar: 'Woman who refused to lie for employer awarded £8,000'.

Rebecca had worked for the same import-export company for ten years as an export executive. Part of her job involved preparing and issuing invoices for orders, sometimes for millions of dollars. She told the industrial tribunal that she had processed bogus invoices worth millions of dollars before realising that they were false, but she had refused to make false depositions to American courts on behalf of her employer. Her allegation was that her employer was creating false business deals as evidence for a lawsuit in America. She felt torn between loyalty to her employer and to God. In her words, 'I'm not a religious fanatic, but I am a practising Christian. I told them I was being put in a position where my loyalty to God and myself was going to clash with my loyalty to them,' she said. 'I felt I was being compromised and I did not want to let anyone down. I can duck and weave but I cannot lie.' Being faced with the prospect of having to give false testimony in American courts felt like 'a locomotive coming down towards the track I was tied on to'.

Rebecca told the tribunal that she had four meetings with her superiors, during which she told them she did not want to lie on the Bible. She defied orders to shred certain documents and instead handed them over to lawyers acting for the American company with whom her own employers were in dispute. She claimed it had been impossible to return to the firm after spilling the beans to lawyers acting for the other side. Her employers claimed she had been given an inducement to claim the documents were forged. The industrial tribunal found that she had been unfairly dismissed and she was awarded £8,000 with costs.

Although the details of this case are complicated and disputed, at the heart of it is the issue of honesty. The newspaper headlines summed it up neatly as a 'Victory for Christian who wouldn't lie'. A Christian lives by the word of God and follows values that are timeless and changeless. For all of us, there is a time when a line must be drawn, whatever the personal cost. Rebecca was being asked to do something which she felt was wrong. She was prepared to stand up and be counted in an industrial tribunal. She laid her Christian convictions firmly on the table. And she won.

In the case I have just described there was a great deal at stake, not least a multi-million dollar lawsuit – but you cannot put a price on personal integrity. What the Christian stands for is, in Jesus's phrase, like a pearl of great price. It is not something to be light-heartedly tossed aside and crushed under the feet of those who live by different rules. It is to be valued and cherished.

THE FOLLY OF THE FIDDLE

The confident Christian will set high standards for the workplace and be aware of the pitfalls that lie ahead. Honesty and integrity are hallmarks of any person of moral principles. For those of us who are Christians, they are doubly important, yet it is not always easy to maintain our values. Take something relatively unimportant, like the claiming of expenses: 'fiddling expenses' is endemic in some professions. One way in which the Christian can stand out is to be honest in all dealings, including expenses. It isn't easy.

I once had my expenses rejected by one manager for not claiming enough! I had claimed train fares to go to one location for a news conference, but as I was carrying technical equipment, I was entitled to go by taxi. I was told that the right to use a cab was a concession that this particular department had fought hard to secure. If I were now to claim train fares and not taxi fares, it would undermine the outcome of a long negotiation. Out of respect for my colleagues, I then always used a cab while I worked for that particular employer. This kind of issue requires fine judgment.

Another tricky area I have encountered is hospitality to clients. Some people invent the names of their lunch guests to make their expenses claim look more legitimate and to impress their line manager. Apart from being dishonest, it is also stupid. Managers are not daft and one question about the conversation you had with your client will betray dishonesty. Of course, if you keep claiming for hospitality to your friends, you may score points for honesty but lose points for exploiting the system. The whole area of expenses is fraught with hazards. It is important to know where the lines are drawn, what you are and are not entitled to claim and then to be scrupulously honest.

THE NOT SO SMART ALEX

Sometimes, the expenses fiddle can turn into a personal nightmare. It did for Alex. He headed up the technical operations department of a large communications company which provided a service to national and international broadcasters. His ability to provide top quality public address systems and to provide facilities for other media anywhere in the world had won him a reputation as a rugged and reliable operator. A tall man in his early fifties, Alex was highly respected amongst his colleagues and seemed set for a dazzling decade as his company headed for a major expansion. His operations had become global, providing technical services to the highest in the land wherever they happened to be. But Alex made a fatal miscalculation. He was impatient for the rewards that come with success and spotted a loophole in the system. His work involved long and unsociable hours and no one really knew what hours he worked. His claims for overtime were never questioned. Alex reckoned that he was badly underpaid for the responsibilities he had, so he started to top up his salary by putting in false overtime claims.

This might have gone unnoticed, had he not become greedy and added to his exaggerated overtime claims for late night taxis to take him to his home in Berkshire. To help cover his tracks, the expenses and overtime claims of some of his staff started to be inflated as well so that Alex's own claims would not stand out too much. He got away with it for over five years. His undoing was the introduction of an outside consultant by his firm to check the books and locate some savings. One of the first things the consultant noticed was that overtime payments were high and that there seemed to be an awful lot of cabs being used through the night. Soon the consultant was looking carefully at Alex's personal expenses and overtime claims.

The consultant was amazed at the hours Alex seemed to be working – and some of those working for him. He decided to contact the cab company to confirm that Alex really had made all those trips home from the office in the early hours. Some of the claims were true, but it became clear, when the taxi firm sent in their records, that not all the times and places tallied with Alex's returns or those of some of his staff. What the consultant had uncovered was a huge overtime fiddle, worth tens of thousands of pounds to Alex and some of his staff over the years. Had it come to court, he could have ended up in jail. As it was, he had a benevolent employer and out of respect for his loyal service over many years and fearful of the bad publicity that could result from his dismissal, Alex was given instant 'early retirement'. The money he had falsely claimed was recouped by his company out of his pension and retirement benefit. He left in disgrace. A dodge had become a fiddle and that was tantamount to fraud.

I tell this story to show how something which began as a small fiddle grew into a monster out of control. The integrity and reputation of a loyal and hard-working man was compromised by dishonesty in a matter that had seemed to him trivial. He left his firm discredited and poorer for it. What Alex had done was clearly wrong, but it was also sheer folly. The consequences of sin live with us and in Alex's case, it has led to an early exit in shame with many years left to him to repent at leisure. Sin can carry a heavy price.

KNOW YOUR ORGANISATION

Confidence at work will be all the more easy as we get to know the kind of organisation we work for. It is a mystery to me that individuals can work for the same firm for many years, yet never get to grips with how their organisation works, or how it thinks. Lack of awareness about the nature of the beast can lead to a sense of dislocation, a feeling that however hard you try, your face simply does not fit. It may be true, but more often than not, failure to understand the culture of an organisation is to blame.

Every company has its own culture and identity. Each has its own pattern of behaviour, its own carefully constructed cobweb of how things are done, who decides what, unwritten rules of acceptable behaviour. The person who blunders in, unaware of the house rules, can quickly become like a bull in a china shop, doing damage at every turn. Companies large and small have norms and rules, rarely written down, that count for a lot. These can range from important issues, such as power structures and chains of command, to seemingly trivial matters such as dress code and how you address your line managers. The confident Christian will make sure these unwritten laws are known and understood.

The first thing an outsider looks at is a company's recruitment literature and annual report. Inevitably these documents will show a company's policies and performance in the best possible light, but even in that process, it is possible to identify the goals of an organisation and how it intends to achieve those targets. If there is much talk of reducing the costs of overheads, for instance, you can be sure that a cost-cutting process is underway with many managers worrying if their jobs are about to be lopped off like the overcrowded branches of an apple tree in need of a good prune.

To feel confident and at home in your workplace certain factors need to be in good order. You need to know the organisation you work for – its values, its systems, its expectations of you. You need to have a sense of your own place within it, and you need to bring into it the 'added value' of your own beliefs and standards as a Christian. These should be an asset, a commitment to honest dealing, sensitivity to people, a care and concern to do a good job and to do it well.

UNRAVELLING THE CULTURE

In a small organisation, there are no secrets. If the boss arrives in a foul mood and snaps at the assistant, the chances are that the rest of the firm will know about it pretty fast. With the ability of computers to talk to one another, others might get the message (literally) within moments of an outburst of temper. I have sat in a meeting addressed by a company director and watched one of his staff sending a message of disdain to a colleague across the room, rubbishing what had just been said.

In a large corporate organisation the ethos and 'feel' of an organisation can be very pronounced. But that unwritten code of conduct can change from one department to another. When I left the *Today* programme, where I had been a producer, to work for the then BBC Foreign News Intake department, my new job was based in the newsroom in London's Broadcasting House. The job was to co-ordinate the BBC's foreign news correspondents, commission despatches and move correspondents around to cover the big stories of the day. It was the mid-eighties, and it was unusual at that time to switch from current affairs to the newsroom. News and current affairs were two different worlds and crossover of staff was comparatively rare. Most people in the newsroom wore jacket and tie for day shifts and casual clothing for night shifts and weekends. So when I went over to meet my colleagues in the television newsroom, I went in my suit and tie to attend their morning news meeting. I soon became aware that everyone was looking at me oddly and that I stuck out like a sore thumb. In television, jacket and tie had long been confined to the dustbin and informality was the house style. Once I removed my tie, I felt far more comfortable and blended in.

That was a very trivial event which happened a long time ago, but it makes the point about being aware of the culture. Nowadays, news and current affairs are a single directorate within the BBC and interchangeability of staff is the order of the day, so that experience would not happen now.

Some firms have a system of 'mentors' – old lags who can help the newcomer to settle in by telling them the do's and don'ts of the organisation. If these don't exist it may be helpful to have an early drink with a friendly colleague. Who's in, who's out, quirks of your department, what is liked and disliked, how to dress, how strict time-keeping is, what allowances can and cannot be claimed, what constitutes an own goal – all of this is essential in the office survival kit. Does your place of work have a paper mentality, or are communications electronic? Is the best means of communication a word in a colleague's ear, a memo in triplicate, or a message logged into the computer? Again this can vary within the organisation.

The biblical example epitomising the good employee is the Old Testament character of Joseph. He was fiercely loyal to God and to his employer and maintained his personal integrity. Joseph had to resist the temptation offered by Potiphar's wife who was seeking a sexual liaison with him. The book of Genesis can be disarmingly frank at times. 'Now Joseph was well-built and handsome, and after a while his master's wife took notice of Joseph and said, "Come to bed with me!"' Joseph refused. His reply is a case study in diplomacy. '"My master has withheld nothing from me except you, because you are his wife. How then could I do such a wicked thing and sin against God?"' (Gen. 39: 6–7, 9) She carries on pestering him in an early example of sexual harassment, seizes his clothes one day, and poor Joseph ends up in prison. But even there he finds favour and slowly works his way back into influence, using his God-given power of dream interpretation to make himself indispensable to Pharaoh.

So it is always a good idea to find out early on how best to communicate within the culture of the organisation you work for. The ability to interpret dreams served Joseph well. For us it is more likely to be interpreting other abilities! If you start sending off memos in all directions within a few days of arriving in a culture that is computerate or relies on word of mouth, you will quickly acquire the reputation of being a pedantic dinosaur or on some kind of power trip.

When you are a newcomer it's so easy to go wrong. One blunder I made seriously undermined my confidence and nearly cost me a job as producer of Radio 4's *Today* programme. I was 'on attachment' – a six-month secondment from the BBC World Service to the *Today* programme. I had only been there a few weeks when a vacancy suddenly emerged on *Today*, leaving me perfectly placed to secure it. But with stunning naivety and stupidity, I did not apply for it. I was not seeing clearly. The programme editor was aghast that I wasn't going for the job and suggested very strongly that I should apply. Despite his heavy hints, I was still feeling unsure of myself, had not yet settled in and so did not apply for the vacancy.

Weeks later when the job was filled, I saw my folly. By then it was too late. As my six-month attachment drew to a close, I was destined to return to my old job. I was not happy. The programme editor extended my attachment, but unless one of the current team of producers left, I was out. Fortunately for me, one of *Today*'s producers was recruited by a then unknown new breakfast television company called TV-AM. God was very good to me. This created an opening on *Today*. I had learned my lesson, went for the job and got it.

POWER STRUCTURES

As we get to know our employer and the funny ways of the firm for which we work, we settle in and grow in confidence. It's always useful to know where power lies within an organisation and who makes the decisions. In a large organisation, this may be so many levels above that you feel like an ant on a football pitch, with the power brokers somewhere in the stratosphere. It's useful to know how you fit in.

An obvious starting-point is your company's organisation chart. This won't tell you who meets whom for lunch, or which managers are related to each other, but it's a beginning. Power may rest in the boardroom or in the top company executives. It may be the case that it's at lower levels where the real influence is exercised – by those who control how budgets are put together or spent. Some people may have little power but a lot of influence. So if you know who you can go to to talk through ideas, to test the waters and in what order you should approach the people from whom you need support, it all helps. You also need an insider who can tell you who prefers to speak to staff in person and who prefers to receive memos.

Where careful lines of management have been established, it is important to work through them and not leap-frog your line managers. Going above the head of your immediate boss to the next layer smacks of disloyalty and can be one of those killer mistakes which can wreck your relationship with your boss. From a Christian point of view, loyalty and support for your boss are important qualities. Take Jesus's parable of the talents. It is the servant who puts the talents he is given to good effect, increasing their value, who is praised and rewarded. 'You have been faithful with a few things; I will put you in charge of many things,' says the master (Matt. 25: 21). Jesus has more than one layer of meaning here. This is not just about being a good employee and using the talents we have to best effect, but it is also a lesson for life. What God has given us, he wants us to use.

In Luke's Gospel in the parable of the shrewd manager,

Jesus tells the story of a manager facing the sack for wasting company resources. In the end, the shrewd manager decides to cut his losses, recouping much of his master's debts and is commended for acting shrewdly. 'Whoever can be trusted with very little can also be trusted with much, and whoever is dishonest with very little will also be dishonest with much' (Luke 16: 10). Loyalty, honesty and wisdom are core values of the confident Christian at work and we do well to remember just how important they are.

If there are issues you wish to raise at a higher level, let your line manager know before you start stirring muddy waters. Almost certainly she or he is better placed than you are to raise the issue.

SURVIVING OFFICE POLITICS

I was once sent on a week's management training course to learn one lesson: the importance of 'networking' within a large organisation. The course leaders wanted to instil into us the importance of having a friend within the organisation who understands its culture but who is outside our own department. Such a person can be invaluable for off-loading frustrations, talking through problems and seeing your situation through different eyes. A colleague of mine in television is particularly skilled at networking. He uses the famous 'canteen lunch' as his test-bed for office politics. Others prefer the cup of coffee in the Italian café down the road, finding more freedom outside the office buildings.

Most work situations include a degree of what is usually called 'office politics', i.e. the whole business of getting on, and Christians are not immune to it. There will be those who will seek to exploit the specific situation to further their career, or to be seen to do well, often to the detriment of others. Many departments in organisations, or even in small working units, may have their fair share of 'back-stabbers', who are nice to your face but rubbish your work behind your back. Then there are the 'brown-noses', who are the types who suck up to their bosses and will do anything to keep in their good books – those who will do anything to please their masters. I have to admit that this side of working in a close-knit environment can be very demanding of the Christian. Indeed I have heard one non-Christian colleague describe it as 'black art', suggesting that you need to be Machiavellian or devious to succeed.

THE PERILS OF NAIVETY

The first mistake a confident Christian should avoid at all costs is that of naivety: more easily said than done. The story I am about to tell still causes me to wince.

I was a new boy still cutting my teeth as a producer for the news organisation for which I was then working. The editor of the news programme was an outstanding journalist, a terrific team leader called Steve. His enthusiasm, drive and acumen was matched only by his dazzling personality and popular appeal. This went beyond the confines of the office into the bedroom of one particularly attractive production assistant elsewhere in the department, called Susie. When you work overnight on a programme, the editor needs to be available at home for consultation. Stories might break of which the editor should be aware. Difficult editorial decisions may have to be taken which need to be referred upwards to your editor.

I have no recollection now of why I needed to contact Steve, but I did. There were two numbers on the office telephone list – that of his wife and that of Susie. I rang the first number on the list. 'Is Steve there, please?' I asked. 'No, he's not.' Thinking I recognised the voice, I carried on: 'Sorry to disturb you, Susie, it's just that I need to contact him'. There was a long silence. 'This is Steve's wife Mary speaking – WHO IS SUSIE?' I died and quickly ended the conversation – terribly sorry, wrong number, etc.

The next day Steve came in with a face like thunder. 'All right, who's the idiot who rang my wife last night and called her Susie!' He was not a happy man. As for me, I felt like an idiot. This sensitive Christian had just made the most ghastly, tactless and stupid blunder. I apologised profusely and tried to point out to Steve the risk of writing down a girlfriend's home number alongside that of his wife! He had been stupid too. I received a severe dressing-down for being naive and tactless and plunging him into a furious row with his wife. But Steve was also painfully aware that his lifestyle had caught up with him at last. Had he been a vindictive man, it could have set back my career severely. But he was decent and fair to his staff, even though he was cheating on his wife. He put it down to a combination of naivety on my part and carelessness on his, so no lasting damage was done to my career.

I shudder even to recall this incident over ten years later. I hesitated to tell you, so awful was it. With one phone call to the wrong person I had managed to plunge my line manager into the biggest row of his marriage. It was a marriage that I am sad to say did not survive. I'm not saying that what I did led to the break-up – that happened years later – but it certainly didn't help. Needless to say, the episode did not do my confidence much good either. I knew it would take a lot of very good programmes and keeping out of trouble for the painful memory to fade.

If the first problem is naivety, the second is to find yourself slipping and sliding into the prevailing culture. It's all too easy to join in the gossip about the boss or the newest member of staff. We all want to be liked and can find ourselves going out of our way to please our line managers. If we are not careful we start to compromise where we should be standing our ground. The difficulty for the Christian is how to avoid slipping into the prevailing traps. To employ tactics such as using gossip, slander, back-stabbing or brown-nosing the boss to get on, is simply not an option. As Christians we are called to 'Live as children of light (for the fruit of the light consists in all goodness, righteousness and truth) and find out what pleases the Lord' (Eph. 5: 8–10).

A CHRISTIAN APPROACH

So the tactics of the Christian in a highly political or sensitive working environment will be to deploy a distinctly Christian approach. This will mean using your integrity and honesty to the advantage of yourself and the gospel. There is a phrase used by Jesus when he sent out his disciples on their first assignment which I have always found very helpful. It is both immensely subtle and quite uncompromising. Jesus sends us out 'like sheep among wolves. Therefore be as shrewd as snakes and as innocent as doves' (Matt. 10: 16).

What a powerful combination of qualities that is. We should keep our innocence, being as pure as doves, but we should not be fools either, burying our heads in the sand. We are to be as shrewd as snakes, wary of our vulnerability, but equipped with our Christian morality and principles to survive and indeed to prosper. It is with those qualities at the back of our minds that we approach the complexities of work relationships.

I do have some misgivings at suggesting exactly how a Christian should use these qualities. For some of my Christian brethren, the advice would be to steer well clear of a particular friendship and to be 'above it'. I'm all for seizing the high ground on business morality and ethics, but to think you can do so without encountering office politics is in my view naive, if not foolhardy.

BLUNDERS AND PITFALLS

Office politics can be a minefield and the pitfalls are too many to imagine. Not being aware of some colleague's personal situation, not knowing who is sleeping with whom, inadvertently passing on something told to you in confidence, accidentally sending a sensitive document to the wrong person, discussing one's salary in front of others who may be earning more or less – all of these are potential hazards.

None of us can guarantee not to drop some clanger. We are always learning and the next mistake may be only minutes away. It pays to keep on your guard and think before you act. If you are in a sensitive situation, pray about it. Prayer is a vital resource for the Christian, as we shall see in the next chapter. So what, then, are those lethal errors that can set back both our confidence and our career? Let's not forget that blunders like these can not only bring us into disrepute, but, more damaging still, they can damage our Christian witness. Therefore we can find that we are not only letting down ourselves, but also our colleagues and our faith.

Blunders can be killers, and some mistakes are more deadly than others. The worst of these is to go over the head of your boss to prove some point, or to boost your own image in the organisation. Loyalty is a much-prized asset and is the other side of the coin to trust. If you are disloyal to your closest colleagues, can you be trusted? Trespassing on other people's 'turf' is another sure way to make enemies and irritate your colleagues. Being too pushy and constantly name-dropping is a social sin that might impress the impressionable but won't fool the wise. It goes alongside boasting, humiliating others, talking about personal wealth and crawling to the bosses as sure-fire routes to disaster. As the book of Proverbs puts it, 'Haughty eyes and a proud heart, the lamp of the wicked, are sin! The plans of the diligent lead to profit as surely as haste leads to poverty. A fortune made by a lying tongue is a fleeting vapour and a deadly snare' (Prov. 21: 4–6).

THE JOKE THAT BACKFIRES

The last of the lethal blunders is the joke that explodes in your face. We can never be too careful about our sense of humour. Jokes can easily be misunderstood and dry humour misinterpreted as serious comment. I have inherited from my mother a heavy sarcasm and it has landed me in all kinds of trouble. A reporter had done a not very good piece of journalism. I was asked to comment. 'For you, not bad at all!' I say with a touch of sarcasm. 'What do you mean, not bad – what's wrong with it?' responds now angry reporter. Whoops! That kind of situation is irritating and entirely my own fault, but it can be smoothed over quickly.

Dave was in his early thirties and considered a high flier

in his department. He was intellectually sharp, with a tongue like a razor, quick to put colleagues in their place with a rapier-like wit that cut through pomposity and phoney argument. But the career of this particular high flier landed with a bump because he could not resist sarcastic comments at his colleague's expense. Unknowingly he had offended his head of department with a cutting comment. As Proverbs wisely puts it, 'The words of a man's mouth are deep waters, but the fountain of wisdom is a bubbling brook . . . A fool's lips bring him strife, and his mouth invites a beating' (Prov. 18: 4, 6).

I know that my dry humour and corny puns have often been misunderstood as serious comments. If you have a sense of humour, take care how you use it. You can damage your own standing with a tactless comment, an insensitive suggestion, or sarcasm that can all too easily be interpreted as cynicism. I've had to curb my outspokenness at times because it would only have made my life harder. Some of us can be too blunt for our own good.

When John, the writer of the fourth Gospel, described Jesus's character, he saw him as full of grace *and* truth. That is the perfect balance. The Christian can sometimes be all truth and no grace, coming across as a dogmatic cold fish, uncaring and tactless. Or you can be all grace and no truth, full of sympathy and smooth as silk, but lacking in conviction. Grace and truth go together for the confident Christian like bacon and eggs. No one earns the respect of colleagues more quickly than the person who is fair, gracious and straightforward. One Christian friend has risen to the top of her organisation in this way – by being enthusiastic in her work, maintaining her Christian integrity and being brilliant with people, always finding time for them and being positive in outlook.

We have seen that office politics can be exceedingly dangerous. It's better to keep yourself well informed with a good network of friends around the organisation, but largely uninvolved in the power games. The danger zones to be avoided at all costs by Christians are back-stabbing, false promises and spreading rumours. The apostle James knew all about the dangers of careless talk. 'The tongue is a small part of the body, but it makes great boasts. Consider what a great forest is set on fire by a small spark. The tongue also is a fire, a world of evil among the parts of the body' (Jas. 3: 5–6).

If, on the other hand, we are able to be the peacemaker, the reconciler, the mediator in situations that are tense, it will be noticed. If every Christian worker was to make this the abiding standard and quality of his or her work, then what a difference it would make. A team-worker who puts others first and mends hurts is an angel. It is possible to have this kind of influence in the workplace. When we go for it, it is noticed. Good practice does get noticed by others.

COPING WITH FAILURE

Every person at some stage in their career can expect to face the Big Letdown. This is a great setback, either missing the promotion we thought was in the bag, or worse, being told we have no future or that the company is 'letting us go'. When it happens, however well we might explain it to ourselves, it hurts really badly. And as we get older, it hurts even more. Even if our job is reasonably secure, it is still very tough when we hit what is known as the glass ceiling and find our promotion blocked.

Curiously, experiencing the bitter taste of failure can increase our self-confidence, if we handle it in the right way. Failure is, after all, a key test of self-confidence, just as handling life when things go wrong is a truer test of faith than the good times. Faith worth having can cope with the tough times. Confidence rooted in faith is tested not in the warm glow of success but in the chill frost of failure.

A friend of mine, Frances, went through such an experience. She was in line for a promotion, waiting for her manager to move on. They had been an effective team working together and when her boss was promoted, she hoped to succeed him. But, as can often happen in open competition, the post went to the outside candidate, not to

Confidence at Work

the incumbent. It was a painful experience for Frances. She found she couldn't sleep properly and she felt angry with God. During these tumultuous days she kept a diary to organise her thoughts and feelings. Here is an extract:

> Yesterday was very long. I came out of the selection panel confident the job was mine. But it was hours before I was summoned to learn the outcome. As I walked into the room, the chairman of the panel was smiling. He said how well I had done and how the decision had been agonisingly close. Just as I expected him to tell me the job was mine, he dropped the bombshell. I hadn't got it. Someone else was being given the job. I felt sick in the pit of my stomach. I found it hard to take in. How could I have failed? I felt numb and shocked. I wasn't angry then, just disbelieving. I wanted to get out of that room fast but was desperate to hear an explanation that I could grasp. That another candidate had done better did not help. I guess I just wasn't prepared for the awful reality of failure. An overwhelming sense of injustice hit me like a tidal wave. The day after was worse. By now I was in the full throes of feeling rejected even though my colleagues were very supportive – some seemed more upset than I was – I could sense my emotions grappling with what had happened – a mix of anger, resentment and confusion abounded.

Twenty-four hours and one broken night's sleep later, Frances takes up her story:

> I slept badly. In my dreams I was reliving my selection panel and arguing with every member on it. I could not believe they could turn me down. When I woke I recognised what I was feeling from a long forgotten experience buried deep in my subconscious. I struggled for a while to identify what it was I was feeling. Then my memory dredged it up from some dark abyss in my mental memory bank. I remembered how years earlier I had been mugged. Some drunken youth had punched me and split my lip. Hospital casualty had stitched it up. I had

felt then a mix of powerlessness and physical hurt. This morning I felt just the same, as if I had been mugged by my employer. I was hurting inside and felt badly let down. My trust and confidence had been bulldozed. Tomorrow I will feel better but today I feel sorry for myself and cheated. I'm not angry with the bloke who did get the job, he must have done pretty well.

Frances had the good sense not to let feelings of sorrow stop her from doing her job. She resisted the temptation to slope off early or come in late the next day. A colleague told her that he had been 'dead impressed'. For the Christian in this situation there is another dimension. Where is God in all of this? What of all the prayer that has gone up? God is not deaf or blind, he is working out his own goals in this which may or may not coincide with our own. This is where the promise of a God who in all things, 'works for the good of those who love him' (Rom. 8: 28), is a great strength and comfort.

TRYING TO MAKE SENSE OF IT

Hard though it is, it is essential in this situation to hang on to the bigger picture, the sense that in God's purposes, another game is being played, another purpose worked out. Failure can be a liberation. Crucial to this whole process is the ability to separate the situation from ourselves. Failure to get a job or to achieve a goal is usually not a commentary on us personally or a calculated attack on our self-esteem, though it will seem like it. The reality is that we are not our job or our status or a three-word description of ourselves. I am I and you are you. Failure or success may seem to impact upon our self-esteem, but that is a matter of perception, not of reality. Our self-worth rests on other things, not on one job selection interview or its outcome.

Let's look a little at what is going on during a trauma of this sort. There are various stages that we go through, well documented by those who make a study of these things.

HOW WE REACT TO A CRISIS

There are four basic stages that those who experience unexpected change can expect to go through. It doesn't matter whether it is failure to get a job, a breakdown in a relationship, an accident to a loved one, or a sudden change in circumstances. If it happens to you and affects you deeply, then it will be traumatic to some degree. These are times to learn about ourselves through the process of change. It may well be that our sense of self-esteem takes quite a battering and we feel ourselves pulled through life's wringer. Again, we must distinguish the situation from the person, if we can.

SHOCK

First there is the shock. This goes hand in hand with a sense of disbelief. It can't be happening; it can't be true; it can't be happening to me. You feel crushed with the immensity of what has happened. Curiously, as you question what has taken place, there is sometimes a surge of energy and perhaps even a sense of excitement. You know that the Rubicon has been crossed, that your life has been touched or changed in a way that you cannot control. This is your body building up your defences for the full impact of the changes about to hit you like a sledgehammer.

DESPAIR

After the shock and disbelief comes the low point. This is the second stage. You are now aware that the unexpected change is likely to be a permanent one. Much as you might like to turn back the clock, you can't. It has happened. You feel very low. Your confidence begins to ebb away. Despair may not seem very far away, but you are comforted by the perverse thought that it cannot get any worse than it feels right now. You feel sorry for yourself and feel bad about that! This is the dangerous point, too, when many people will turn to drink and try to drown their sorrows. Alcohol, however, is a depressant and will often make these feelings of despondence even worse. Here is the point for the Christian to be sure to carry on praying. God shares in our pain and our sadness, and does not want to be excluded from it.

The feelings of distress and disappointment sap our energy and our confidence very badly. We feel a bit like a bag of peanuts left out for the birds in winter. It's as if the bluetits are pecking at the peanuts, and you can almost physically sense your self-confidence being chipped away as you grapple to come to terms with the new situation. You are grasping the fact that you need to change to face the change forced upon you. The reality begins to dawn that you cannot go on as before. There will be adjustments and decisions to make. You become more introspective and reflective, trying to find keys from the past to unlock your understanding.

COMING ROUND

The third stage – after the immediate shock and disbelief and the self-doubt – is facing up to the new reality. This is the stage when you let go of the past and start to face the future. It becomes clear that you cannot stand still: you must move on to whatever lies ahead. You begin to work through your feelings again. Maybe the change isn't quite as bad as it first seemed. There is light appearing at the end of the tunnel. With the change has come the opportunity to shape the future. You're not feeling sorry for yourself in the same way now, you can begin to look beyond the next day to a more distant future. In fact, you wish events would speed up a bit, so you can start to move forward to whatever does lie ahead. It's as if you've been released from a darkened room and your eyes are adjusting to the brightness of the daylight.

MAKING THE CHANGE

The fourth stage is making the adjustment. We have travelled through the initial shock and pain. We have felt sorry for ourselves and examined ourselves to try to understand where we went wrong, or where events overtook our control. We have been through the letting go phase and the coming to terms with the new realities. Our mind has already started to put a toe in the new waters, to test the temperature. We are anxious to see what the future holds and a feeling of irritation and impatience has come into play. Now comes the adjustment.

At last the new situation begins to make sense and we can reflect on how things have changed. We have decided that even if we cannot agree with or fully comprehend what has taken place, we can live with it. It may mean a change in behaviour, it may affect our working patterns and our lifestyle, it may throw up new routines to replace the old. Whatever it means, the fact is that we are now looking forward and not looking back. The pain has dulled and our confidence has come through – dented but intact. We are now ready to face the future. The search for God's guidance and for meaning takes on a new urgency. Despair has gone, there is the beginning of hope and of the search for what is to come. God's great unknown beckons.

3
THE CONFIDENT COLLEAGUE

Malcolm had a naturally abrasive personality. At his best he was an inspiration to his staff, but at his worst he knew just what to say to get under their skin and make them loathe him. Linda was a gentle woman and she could not stand any more of Mal's sharp tongue and rapier sarcasm. Relationships between them were so strained that they could barely talk to each other. It was infecting the whole office team like gangrene. One of the team was a Christian called Humphrey. He decided to take it in hand himself and act as a go-between. He explained Malcolm's style to Linda and told Malcolm that Linda was sensitive to his jibes. Only an apology from Malcolm to Linda would do and Linda in turn had to swallow her pride and say 'sorry' for over-reacting.

The confident Christian aims to be a positive influence in the workplace – a team-player who adds to the mix. In the Sermon on the Mount, Jesus compared the Christian to salt and to light (Matt. 5: 13–16). Salt adds flavour; it preserves what is good and stops it going rotten, which is why meat was salted in the age before the refrigerator. Just a pinch of salt can make a whole barrel-load of difference to how something tastes. The Christian in the workplace is to be the person who adds flavour to it. That gives it a pleasant taste and keeps what is good from decay and deterioration.

The Christian is also 'light', showing up darkness for what it is. Jesus suggested in the Sermon on the Mount that the place for a lamp is on a lampstand. It can no more be hidden than a city on a hill. So our light is to shine out before others, 'that they may see your good deeds and praise your Father in heaven' (Matt. 5: 16).

BECOME A PROBLEM SOLVER

One way in which that light can shine and cut through the darkness is to become the office problem solver. In any office there will be personality clashes. Become the peacemaker everybody trusts. Recognise that everyone is different and has their own contribution to make. As the one who scatters light, you can show the way to unlocking the personalities and seeing how they can work together like different-shaped pieces of a jigsaw. In a creative environment there is often an explosive mix of conflicting temperaments – creative people can also be volatile, passionate, not necessarily articulate and at times frustrating. Some people are like plants, constantly coming up with the seeds of new ideas, but quite unable to focus their attention on which ideas will work and which are hopeless. The problem solver is a key player in any team.

A West London YMCA has a chief executive who is as near as you can get to a professional problem solver. She is one of those rare people who overflow with ideas. She thinks laterally and has that ability to combine two apparently unconnected ideas into a winning formula. That's why in January, the local YMCA holds a ball. It's a treat to dress up and have a really posh night out, with a dinner and dance in your finest outfit. Christians also like to support the work of organisations like the YMCA. Solution? Lay on a high quality dinner/dance evening at the local hotel. Persuade the hotel to provide a quality meal at a heavily discounted price. Charge lots for a double ticket and tell supporters to bring along their friends and book a table for ten. That way the YMCA can raise a substantial amount of money, support local business (the hotel) and give their supporters a good evening out, all in one fell swoop. The best ideas are those that are both simple and effective. How does this clever lady do it? 'I don't see walls,' she told me. She has the gift of seeing solutions rather than difficulties and so achieves her goal whatever seems to stand in the way. She sees it as the best use of her God-given creative abilities as part of a team.

To be a confident Christian in the workplace there are a few things we need to know that will keep us on top of problems as they occur. We have seen that Christians are to be shrewd as serpents but gentle as doves (Matt. 10: 16), and wisdom at work means being streetwise. Tackling problems requires the ability to break them down into bite-sized chunks, so that we can deal with them.

HOW TO ANALYSE A PROBLEM

Have you a problem that needs to be solved? First, let's see if we can try to define what the problem is, drawing on our experience and intuition to establish why things are not right and where they are going wrong. It might be the way in which things are done – some method or office practice that isn't up to it. Or the problem may revolve around personalities, or perhaps one person not pulling their weight. Maybe it's a colleague who's become a loose cannon on the deck, or someone not understanding their role. Is this a serious problem, or will it go away and resolve itself with time? Is there an obvious solution or a person clearly suited to deal with it?

Secondly, why not see if we can come up with the solution, steering our team towards it, being flexible and able to change course when necessary. Progress on one problem might help us with another. Brainstorming with our team might help to establish the solution and to win around those needed to make the chosen solution work. This is especially true in cases where a change in working method is our solution and it needs everyone to support that adjustment.

Thirdly, let's go for the fast route to goal and tackle the problem itself. Aim to solve it, not to paper over the cracks. Once action is taken, then it will rapidly become clear whether or not the problem is solved. Either way, we will learn new information about the problem which may in itself reveal more solutions – or problems. If there is a pile of snow outside our front door, we can sit and wait for it to melt, or we can go to the garden shed, reach for the shovel and start digging. Action will bring about a quicker solution than inaction. If we leave it alone to go away, the problem might resolve itself, or it might come back to haunt us.

The fourth step is to keep an eye on the problem – to review the situation. If we look for links among the different problems we are dealing with, we might find a way through. Some problems are interrelated, linked by a common flaw in procedure or lack of resources. If the problem remains unsolved, then we need to redefine it, to take a fresh look by perhaps calling in outside help. The problem may be so close to us that we cannot see it. We might be the problem ourselves.

It is worth saying that not all of us will be able to work through complex problems in an original way. Some people can think laterally and see solutions better than others. But every Christian has the ability to be a positive force for reconciliation between people. It is part of our role in society. Not everyone is a natural problem solver. Many of us find it hard to think of clever strategies, new ways to solve a problem. But all of us can play a role in contributing to a solution, if only by stimulating others to see the problem from different perspectives.

Becoming log-jammed into old thinking is a risk we all take. We can all too easily find ourselves locked into recycling old solutions for new problems. This is often the case in churches, where funds have to be raised, perhaps for a building project. There follows the familiar sequence of jumble sales, buy-a-brick campaigns and the giant thermometer posted outside the church that always looks well short of its target. How demoralising that must seem to those who pass by! One local church near where we live adopted a more modern approach. They called in a professional fund-raiser. This man earned his salary by raising the money from the congregation and local business. Whatever the rights and wrongs of this approach, it illustrates a new solution to an old problem.

APPLYING THE POWER OF PRAYER

There is a danger that we Christians sometimes slip into a mentality that puts a straitjacket around God. We start to think that God is only interested in the big issues and not the small details of our lives. Jesus's stark reminder to his followers that God is so interested in the fine details of our lives that even the hairs on our head are numbered should be a powerful reminder to us, too, of how much God cares for us. He is a God who breaks the chains we try to put around him when we limit what he can do by our lack of prayer and imagination. The fact is that God will get involved in any area of our life at all, even the minutiae. In my job, you'd be amazed how many programme scrapes have been rescued by prayer. When I was working as a producer on *Today* on Radio 4, not a programme would go by without some potential crisis. This often involved two contributors who were expected to arrive at the same time in local radio studios not being there with thirty seconds to go. I found myself using the news bulletins as times to collect my thoughts, to run through the next section of the programme and to pray through any potential hazards.

The tricky meeting, the awkward encounter, the person who promised you some vital document and lets you down, the crucial meeting you have coming up and you're stuck in a traffic jam – all are meat and drink for prayer. It's a resource that is a vital part of the Christian's office equipment. But it's no use at all if it's not brought into play throughout the day.

My wife Gill has been training to become a secondary school teacher while I've been writing this book. Her first teaching practice was, not unnaturally, very demanding. She tells me that many times before facing a new class or a particularly ferocious one, she has taken a few minutes before the start of the class to commit the next forty minutes to God. Sometimes she's found herself praying for specific children with learning or behaviour difficulties. Prayer is effective and does make a difference. A tricky situation becomes manageable after prayer.

ORGANISING YOURSELF AND OTHERS

There are four reserves available to every worker to enable us to do our job: resources, people, time and money. In most situations, we are supplied with the resources we need, but what counts is how we manage them.

What are the things that waste time at work? Getting together with some colleagues, I put together quite an impressive list of time-wasters. In my case it is interruptions, phone calls, colleagues engaging in small talk – all distractions, albeit often pleasant ones. Others talked about routine but unimportant meetings, chasing loose ends, reading paperwork, meeting what turn out to be phoney deadlines set by managers chasing their own tails, lack of priorities. Another grouse was letting long-term projects carry on long after their usefulness had expired.

My wife used to work for a government research department. One of her tasks was to look at the impact of the new county boundaries. When the project began, it seemed a useful and important piece of research, but by the time the data was collected, the information analysed and the conclusions reached, the world had moved on. It was received, read, noted and filed away. After putting a year of her professional life into this project, Gill felt flat and demoralised at the end of it. No wonder. A feeling that our work has no real benefit or in-built satisfaction can be very disheartening.

CONTROLLING PAPER

So much of our confidence is generated from the sense within us that we are in control of our working life, that we have objectives and are getting somewhere. For some people, nothing undermines that more quickly than coming into work and finding their desk covered with heaps of paperwork. In your job there may be different pressures. Our heart sinks and sometimes we seem to be drowning. If paper is your problem then learning to tackle the flow is very important for morale and confidence.

I used to use the familiar three-tray system of 'In', 'Pending' and 'Out'. I've replaced this with a four-tray system which incorporates the 'Urgent? Important?' principle. The top tray is marked 'A' for Action. I look at the 'A' tray every day and it doubles as an 'In' tray.

Papers that can wait go into the 'B' tray – important but not urgent. Papers that I might want to retain for reference, but are not urgent or important, such as changes of phone number or appointments in other departments, go into the 'C' tray. This I look at occasionally, perhaps every six weeks or so, and most of this can then be binned as no longer of any relevance. The fourth tray is a simple 'Out' tray.

The best way of handling paper is to touch it only once. Read, assimilate and then file or throw away. I wish I could be that ruthless, but I am a squirrel by nature, so tend to hang on to papers longer than I ought to. People like me need to be more efficient with paper. I have a colleague who has never been able to handle all the paperwork attached to his job as an outside broadcast producer. His desk has become invisible under indecipherable piles which never decrease and threaten to overwhelm. When he sees this mass of paperwork piling up, he feels overwhelmed by the task before him, like a hedgehog about to cross a motorway.

THE PERSONALITY CLASH

Within any office there will be tensions and difficulties. There will also be those who, however pleasant on their own, simply do not hit it off working together. Few things are as disruptive to office life or to a good atmosphere than the personality clash. When two people who do not get on have to work closely together, mayhem can result. No one is immune.

The broadcasting business is packed with creative people with strong personalities. Clashes are inevitable. A large department can absorb this and certain 'difficult' people can be kept apart with the help of skilful rota-making by the managers. But in a small department, everyone has to be able to get on and this is where problems occur. Nothing saps your confidence faster than a colleague telling you that you are a congenital idiot! It's easy to tell if you have become the butt of the office character assassins. I remember walking into the production office of a programme I had recently joined. The whole room went silent as I entered. It was obvious that I had interrupted a conversation about myself. All the telltale signs were there – red faces, people looking away and an atmosphere you could cut with a knife. It was obvious to me, too, who the number one office assassin was. It was the first person who spoke. 'Hi Justin, how are you?' came the rather too easy welcome. I had identified the person who most resented my sudden arrival.

They all knew that I knew what was going on, but I decided that the last thing I needed at this stage was a personality clash with a resentful colleague. So in this case, my tactic was to defuse the clash by ignoring the cold shoulder and, whatever else happened, not to leave the room. I headed towards the first friendly face I could see and started a different conversation. The gossip then frittered away like dandelion seeds in the wind. After a few weeks in that office, as the staff got to know me and realised I was not the incompetent outsider they had first feared, the gossip continued to fade as I began to build a track record of my own. So my confidence grew. If I walked in again and met a sudden burst of silence, I would say with a smile on my face: 'Talking about me were you? Sorry to interrupt, but I just wanted to say . . .' This puts the plotters firmly in their place!

What do we do, however, about the person with whom we simply cannot get on? How do we overcome the serious personality clash, the person who is undermining us and making our life hell? This is a tougher proposition. The problem may go very deep and be out of our control. What can we do if one of our colleagues feels threatened by us or feels that we intend to make changes to which that person is deeply opposed? Or what if it is just a terrible clash of style, where one person's jokes are taken as personal barbs or where there is a fundamental difference of approach to a project?

RESOLVING CONFLICT

The ability to resolve conflict successfully is probably one of the most important interpersonal skills a Christian can possess. We see a good example in the early church where there is a mega clash of personalities. Imagine having to deal with an argument between Jesus's disciple Peter and the apostle Paul! Can you picture how traumatic it must have been for the church leaders at the Jerusalem Council to see two giants of the early church in direct conflict? Acts Chapter 15 tells the story and Galatians Chapter 2 records Paul's feelings. In his words, 'When Peter came to Antioch, I opposed him to his face, because he was clearly in the wrong' (Gal. 2: 11). The issue was the sorting out of Peter and Paul's respective ministries and Peter's treatment of Gentile Christians. He was avoiding their company at meals. The problem solver was James, the brother of Jesus.

AVOIDANCE AND DEFUSION

James tackled the problem head-on. He did not use the first tactic of problem resolution, which is avoidance. Avoiding a problem can be a valid approach, if the problem is relatively trivial. This is the approach which says that this disagreement is over such a trivial issue, that if you ignore it, it will go away and resolve itself. However, we must be sure that the problem really will go away and has not merely been shelved for later.

The second strategy is defusion – taking the heat out of the crisis. This is a delaying tactic, and James did not tackle the problem in this way, either. We can defuse a conflict in the office by resolving some of the minor points, but leaving the major issue unresolved, or we can find a way to delay or postpone the inevitable confrontation to a time that suits us better. For example, if we are ourselves in conflict with our line manager, and our annual appraisal is a month away, it may be better to wait until the appraisal and sort it out then than to have a damaging confrontation now that could lead to an adverse appraisal.

WHEN CONFRONTATION IS INEVITABLE

If the problem is a big one and the personality clash a deep one, then avoidance and defusion will not solve the problem. It will have to be confronted. Confrontation brings the clash to a head. It faces up to the problem and deals with the conflicting issues. Going back to the clash between Peter and Paul, we see James identifying the problem and then coming up with the God-given solution. In this case, Paul was sent off with Barnabas to take the Christian gospel to the non-Jewish nations and Peter was given the task of focussing his efforts on the Jews.

There are two ways of resolving the personality clash when it reaches the confrontation stage. We can negotiate a solution or, if we are in a position of authority, we can impose one. The negotiated solution is always the better option. This is a win-win strategy in which both parties determine the nature of the solution to the conflict. To do this we need to set aside an agreed time to discuss what the problem is. This can be painful. It means being honest and being prepared to listen. Let's face it: a lot of us are good talkers but lousy listeners. The important thing is to sit down and to listen to each other's point of view and agree a way forward. This will almost certainly require give and take on both sides.

I once found myself having to work closely as a producer with a reporter with whom I was not getting on at all well. We were away for a week on a special assignment. Every idea I had, this reporter rubbished. We had a team of people and were not 'gelling' as a team. The atmosphere between us was strained and even simple tasks were becoming difficult. It was clear that if something was not done, the week was going to become increasingly strained and life would be intolerable for all of us. Though I had the support of my line manager, the solution was mine to find. Other members of the team were sent back to base. This was, if you like, a 'power play' in which I used my seniority to change the situation so that I was left to work alone with the reporter. The two of us then agreed a time and place to sit down and talk in an effort to resolve our differences.

For the Christian in this situation, the priority will be to try to achieve a reconciliation, a meeting of minds in which mutual forgiveness and understanding replace feelings of anger or resentment. It will probably involve both parties to the argument having to say 'sorry', which none of us finds easy to do. Sometimes it takes a very special measure of God's grace to do so. In this particular clash I could have used my seniority to insist on doing things my way, but that would have destroyed our working relationship. Instead, we both wanted to work through the problem. It was painful for both of us, but it was a valuable exercise. We both had to make allowances for how we worked, we both told the other what we felt was wrong and what we found intolerable. It really hurt, listening to someone ripping into you.

Some of the criticism was justified, other parts were not. It didn't matter. The result was good. It was a turning point in our working relationship and the conflict was resolved. It also did wonders for the confidence of both of us. We had worked successfully through a conflict that had threatened to undermine our confidence and standing. We both came out winners, even though our pride had taken a battering.

BEING 'UPFRONT' WITHOUT BEING EMBARRASSING

We Christians are sometimes rather unsubtle in our approach. We think that for others to know we are Christians, it is only necessary to wear a fish badge in our lapel or to talk incessantly about the Sunday sermon to our colleagues on a Monday morning. If our workplace has a Christian Union, we make a big play about going to that instead of joining the gang in the local pub for a jar. All of these things have their place – more in a moment – but they miss the point.

We can be most effective as Christians in the workplace

by finding our proper role within the office – to use the old imagery: by being salt and light. We can be effective Christians at work by being available and accessible and resisting the temptations to become cynical, judgmental, or one of the office character assassins.

Part of the sign of being confident is being able to look at the situation we face and to approach it in prayer to find our role within that situation. In an office of high stress and frequent clashes, our call may be to be the team-player, the bridge-builder and therefore the peacemaker. In a ruthless environment where the loudmouths and line-shooters seem to dominate, there will be 'wallflowers' crushed and driven low by the power players. Our role may be to bring the high and mighty back to earth and to raise up the downtrodden and restore their sense of value and self-esteem.

The important point is to be sure of ourselves, confident in the faith we have, in the God we worship and at peace with ourselves. We will not lose our temper when the pressure is on. We will be the ones who notice when one of our colleagues is under great pressure and we will step in to help out. We will be the ones to get the tea round to restore the flagging energies of the hard workers. Kindness and consideration are old-fashioned virtues that will never lose their power to help and to heal.

BEING 'DISCOVERED'

I have always found it a help when colleagues have been taken by surprise to discover that I am a Christian. It's as if a last piece of the jigsaw that is you has been found. Sometimes I imagine they must be thinking to themselves: 'But you seemed such a normal person!' One colleague asked me how I was able to keep my temper and stay calm when others would have lost theirs. 'How are you able to be so strong?' was the question.

'Perhaps it's to do with my faith,' was my reply, pointing this person in the right direction.

'Oh no, it can't be that,' he said, 'it must be something else!'

Again it was the idea that faith is somehow unrelated to real life that was getting in the way. But I was able to go on to say what a difference being a Christian makes.

Those who discover you are a Christian will have their own expectations of you, depending on what they think (rightly or wrongly) a Christian is. If they find you intriguing, respect you and find you interesting, and then discover in conversation with you that you are a Christian, they seem to take your faith far more seriously.

SHOULD WE WEAR THE FISH?

Should we, then, wear our faith on our sleeve, as it were, by pinning a Cross or a fish in our lapel or on our clothing? I don't believe there is a right or wrong answer here. The question is: is it true to us? Can we carry it off? Are we wearing that fish to intrigue our colleagues and provide an opening? Or is it a sign of separation, to give the message: I am different or even better than you? If our motive for wearing one is wrong, take it off.

Symbols are images or emblems which have their own meaning and standing. They do have the power to influence. Symbols can themselves be a driving force that can spur you into action. If someone is wearing a CND pin or an anti-apartheid badge, those symbols are powerful and tell you about that person. So, too, the Cross is a powerful symbol. The power of the fish symbol is that it is also a secret sign, instantly recognisable to Christians, but a curiosity to others. If we wear one, we must be able to explain why. Some Christians like to wear one because the symbol itself helps them to integrate their inner selves with their external actions in the office. For these people, the wearing of a Cross or a fish can be an aid to being themselves.

The fish is one of the earliest images of Christian art. In the underground burial chambers outside Rome, called the Catacombs, the first Christian believers were buried, awaiting the resurrection of the dead. To prevent the tombs from being defaced or destroyed by pagan enemies of the Church, the early Christians used secret symbols to signify that these were Christian burial chambers. These were simple as well as symbolic – anchors, fish, baskets full of loaves and vines with birds pecking at them. There was the Good Shepherd, borrowed from pagan art of the time and given Christian meaning with the image of a shepherd surrounded by his flock. But of all these symbols, the fish was the most powerful.

The Greek letters for the word fish, 'ICHTHUS', were taken as an acrostic for *Iesous CHristos THeou Uios Soter*, meaning 'Jesus Christ of God the Son, Saviour'. This was a secret sign which also sums up the heart of Christian belief and serves as a powerful visual aid to help explain it.

Personally, I do not wear a fish on my office suit or on my blazer. I find that I prefer to rely on ordinary conversation to open up opportunities to talk about my faith, rather than on outward symbols. But I do wear a fish symbol – albeit a red one – on my lightweight summer jacket, where somehow it looks right. I am not self-conscious about it for some reason on this jacket, although its colour stands out and I have been asked about it twice. 'What's that funny little fish represent?' asked one colleague. He is a keen angler and probably thought it was a River Thames Angling Club logo!

'It's an ancient Christian symbol,' I replied, explaining its meaning. The second time I was asked, I gave the same reply. This time the lady said, 'How interesting! I'm a non-practising Jew and I sometimes wear a Star of David necklace'. Hers was a reply of recognition and mutual respect.

As an opening gambit the fish badge has its value and it will also help identify Christians to one another. But we must not start to rely on the wearing of a Cross or a fish for confidence in the workplace. It can be a useful aid to some, but a barrier to be overcome to others. If we see a colleague wearing a CND badge, do we go out of our way to start discussing nuclear disarmament, or do we give them a wide berth? It's worthwhile taking a few minutes to think about how your colleagues will react to a Cross or fish on your clothing. If it's a help, wear one. If it's a barrier, don't wear one. If you're not sure, wear one anyway and test the reactions of your colleagues. There's nothing to stop you wearing one and asking them a week later if they have noticed it and what they think it represents. After all, it is meant to be a talking point.

UPBEAT NOT DOWNBEAT

Many people feel ground down by their jobs. In these days of economic recession, uncertainty and dwindling workforces, it is hardly surprising. It is so easy to become weary and to slip into the critical frame of mind where yesterday becomes a golden era and the future a black hole. Oscar Wilde said that the cynic is a man who knows the price of everything but the value of nothing.

There is nothing more depressing than a disenchanted Christian who is fed up with church, with the job and is weary of life. If Christians lose hope, then what hope is there for others? Hope is the springboard for action. Christians with hope in their hearts can face any situation, overcome any problem, look on the past with thanks in their hearts and look to the future with a smile on their face. 'Hope does not disappoint us,' says Paul, 'because God has poured out his love into our hearts by the Holy Spirit, whom he has given us' (Rom. 5: 5).

The confident Christian is someone who exudes a positive approach to life at work. Difficulties and problems are not insoluble setbacks sent to try us, but they are temporary hitches to be overcome, which in themselves provide new openings and opportunities. How we handle the setbacks can, as we have seen, make a tremendous difference. It is not easy to escape cynicism, which can seep into an office like a sea fog moving stealthily across the ocean waves and silently swallowing up the coastline as it comes ashore. We must not get lost in the fog. By staying positive and upbeat, we can break out of the cynical thinking and stand for something better.

It is true that the perpetually cheerful colleague can be very irritating. I know that one of my weaknesses is my ability to see the funny side of every situation, to make jokes to break the tension. This can be irritating to some people who begin to think you can't take anything seriously. If you seem to treat all of life as a joke, why should your colleagues take your faith as anything more than something else to be laughed about? Sometimes I get it wrong and seem flippant when it would be better to remain serious. There is a time to joke and a time to refrain from joking. At other times, a burst of humour can be a life-saver, relieving the tension of a crisis. Positive attitudes must be matched by sensitivity to the situation and the reactions of those around us.

What should we be working towards as our goal? To be the bridge-builder and peacemaker within our office is within the reach of every Christian who calls upon the resources available to us through God, both in prayer and in the work of the Holy Spirit through us. We should also aim high. How wonderful it would be if it could be said of every believer that the confident Christian is a good colleague, a sensitive listener and a friend in times of need. We should aim to see the positive side of change and resist the cynical brigade. We should try to be open about our faith but not impose it on others, happy to defend it when attacked but not ready to thrust it down the throats of colleagues. The confident Christian at work is good to have around and has something that others find attractive and intriguing. That is our goal. The confident Christian is not secretive or a conspirator, but is open and honest, as transparent as cling film but not as suffocating.

The confident Christian in the workplace is you and me doing our best to get it right, bringing God into every situation and sometimes taking risks. We will make mistakes but we will be honest enough to own up to our failings. Let us resolve before God to be truly ourselves in the workplace and to let God work through us as children of light, not agents of gloom.

To be as effective as we would like, we will want to make the best use of the resources available to us. So now is the time to look in more detail at the God-given resources to help our confidence grow.

4
RESOURCES FOR CONFIDENCE

Confidence comes in all shapes and sizes. Comedy actress Dawn French was featured in a women's magazine article called 'Me and my Size'. Dawn is not a small lady and eats what she wants when she wants and does so without guilt. 'It's all to do with confidence,' she says. 'I do have confidence but I'm not sure why. I think it comes from a happy upbringing where size was never brought into question.'

Lesley Garrett is a leading soprano with the English National Opera. She has a wonderfully exuberant and vivacious personality. I have watched her walk on stage waving to the audience and blowing kisses at an open air concert at Marble Hill in Twickenham, London. Even as a distant dot on a faraway stage her personality stands out, quite apart from her superb voice. She says, 'I used to think my success was all good luck or a happy accident. But now I don't think that, I think I went out and got it'.

We all know, however, how fragile self-confidence can be. On one of my first overseas assignments for the BBC, I was asked to co-ordinate the radio news coverage of a World Economic Summit in Venice for BBC Radio and the World Service. The logistical problems were a nightmare. The White House press corps were on one island, the British on another and the summit itself on a third. I had a team of correspondents scattered on all three. I spent the week criss-crossing the lagoon, sometimes six times a day, trying to make sure that the right reporters were in the right locations to meet deadlines. There was the additional pressure of heavy security. Whenever Presidents Reagan and Mitterrand, Chancellor Kohl and Prime Minister Thatcher got together, security was ultra-tight. When I realised the enormity of the task, my confidence was not exactly brimming over. I was worrying about how I would cope and afraid that the task was beyond me, so I felt anxious before the summit had even begun. My worst fears were realised when I found myself on one island with a pre-recorded tape on another and the *Today* programme anxiously waiting to receive it. At 2 a.m. I had to get a water taxi to ferry me across to retrieve the tape, only to find that the radio studio had closed down for the night. To save my bacon and give the *Today* programme their promised item, I had to return to my hotel room and rewire the phone system so that I could play the tape down my bedroom telephone. I even had to remove a skirting board and rewire the phone socket to make it work! It took two hours to give them a six-minute item. But they got it and it was broadcast in the end. Overcoming the problem gave my confidence a tremendous boost.

When Nigel Mansell quit the Williams team after winning the world motor racing title, he gave a news conference to tell the world why. What he had to say is very revealing: 'Those who know me well understand the importance to success of the human side and the mutual trust, goodwill, integrity and fair play that are the basis of all human relationships. All these issues have suffered in recent weeks.' Here is the third most successful grand prix driver of all time attributing his decision to retire from Formula One motor racing to an apparent breakdown of trust with his team managers. As a driver, Nigel Mansell's confidence had never been higher. But the web of trust with his team had, for whatever reason, eroded away enough for him to quit the team in which he had finally fulfilled his highest ambitions. He had lost confidence in those around him, but not in himself. The next season, as we have seen, he made the transition to IndyCar racing in the USA with great success.

I have seen outwardly confident people crumble before my eyes when faced with a task which would stretch them. Sometimes a simple task can get out of all proportion. Having to give a speech at a wedding, present a paper or lead a discussion at work, or even give a talk at church to the children's group – all such tasks can prove to be traumatic experiences in prospect.

Attitude and approach are vital. People can worry themselves into an early grave. It's like the story of the glass with some water in it. The positive person sees it half-full, the worrier will see it as half-empty. Confidence is a bit like that – our attitude and approach to a problem will affect how we see it. If we can be positive in our approach, our confidence grows and a daunting task can become manageable. If our state of mind is one of worry and concern, then our confidence can evaporate like the morning dew in the sunshine and the task becomes increasingly tough.

DRAWING UPON GOD

How, then, should the Christian approach all of this? As we shall see, confidence comes from within. The most vital resource the Christian can call into play is God himself – the guidance and direction he offers and the peace he gives to those who are willing to put their confidence in him. When Jesus is briefing his followers about how to cope when he has gone, he promises them the help of his own Spirit whom he describes as the Comforter. Then he tells them, 'Peace I leave with you; my peace I give you. I do not give to you as the world gives. Do not let your hearts be troubled and do not be afraid' (John 14: 27).

Those are words that Christians through the ages have found to be sure-footed and reliable. One of the most dramatic examples from the pages of history comes from Tudor England. In the year 1554, Queen Mary reintroduced three old laws against heresy. It was the dawn of a black period in English history, which earned her the nickname 'Bloody Mary'. In the next four years nearly three hundred people were burned to death as heretics, including no less than five bishops of the fledgling Church of England. The most famous victim was Archbishop Thomas Cranmer, who was responsible for writing so much of the *Book of Common Prayer*. Cranmer was 'persuaded' to sign a document renouncing his beliefs, admitting that he had abused his term as Archbishop of Canterbury and saying that he was wrong to have permitted Henry VIII to divorce his wife.

On the day chosen for Cranmer to be burned alive on the stake, it was raining. He was placed on a platform while a Dr Cole preached to him. After the sermon Cranmer prayed in deep penitence. Then to the astonishment of everyone and the fury of his accusers, he publicly revoked everything he had been forced to confess. As the stake was set alight and the flames built up, he held out his right hand which had signed the false confession and placed it in the flames. At the point of hideous death Cranmer was a man at peace with himself and with God.

'GOD'S PENCIL'

One of the most interesting descriptions of the sense of being guided and directed personally by God comes from that remarkable woman, Mother Theresa of Calcutta. As she cares for the dying and destitute in Calcutta, Mother Theresa is used to receiving visitors from all over the world. One of them asked her if she felt she had special qualities. This was her answer.

> I don't think so. I don't claim anything of the work, it is God's work. I am like a little pencil in his hand. That is all. He does the thinking. He does the writing. The pencil has nothing to do with it. The pencil has only to be allowed to be used. In human terms, the success of our work should not have happened, no?

The key to Mother Theresa's daily routine is that she starts the day with prayer. She starts praying at half-past four in the morning. Clearly she is what is known as a lark not an owl.

If we want to discover for ourselves that sureness of touch and certainty of purpose – if our confidence is to be rooted on solid rock and not sinking sand – we could do a lot worse than emulate her. To start moving forward with a spring in our step ready to take on whatever comes along, we must be sure to take two common-sense measures to ensure that we are in a fit frame of mind. We need to be at peace within ourselves and to be sensible about our rest. We probably won't be up as early as Mother Theresa, but the combination of prayer and sleep can pack a powerful punch in the quest for effective Christian living.

FINDING STILLNESS IN THE CHAOS

One of the most interesting features of London Zoo in recent years has been the 'Moonlight World' within the Charles Clore Gallery. This is a section devoted to animals who are nocturnal. In order to let the public see the fruit bats, lemurs and the like fully active and awake, the Zoo has created an underground gallery, where day and night are reversed. The visitor enters a nocturnal world of darkness, and as your eyes adjust a whole new world emerges from the gloom on the other side of glass panels, full of the most exotic and wonderful creatures. Suddenly your eyes catch the wings of the fruit bat wrapping itself around a peach like a mother hugs a small child. The bats move with speed and near silence, giving the viewer a great sense of serenity and stillness amid all the other movements in their world of darkness. They descend in numbers upon the soft fruit and wrap their black silky wings over it like a hundred matadors swirling their capes.

I was fascinated by the 'Moonlight World'. Despite all the activity going on before my eyes, there was an almost tangible quality to the silence. I could not stop myself thinking of this as a picture of prayer. When we are still before God and seek him out, though our bodies be still and our minds at rest, prayer itself is releasing through God's Spirit his power and strength in our lives. There is an inner strength in stillness and quiet. Too often, we don't allow space for prayer in our lives. I know for myself that I fall into the trap of squeezing prayer into tiny crevices of my day or praying while doing something else. This is no substitute for setting aside time to be still before God. If we restrict our times of quiet prayer and meditation, our inner life will suffer.

One of the great fascinations of Richard Foster's landmark book, *Celebration of Discipline*, is the way in which he reminds the twentieth-century Christian of the importance of the great spiritual disciplines, so often squeezed out by the hectic pace of modern living. Meditation, silence, fasting and contemplation are making a comeback, but the way most of us live our lives makes it very hard to find the space for God which would strengthen our inner life and build up our confidence and trust.

The sad truth is that some of us, myself included, prefer to be surrounded by noise and find silence rather disturbing. We perhaps see prayer as an activity that must be squeezed into our daily schedule, which is all too often anything but calm. In our work environment, in our home life, and in our church life too, activity and noise play a prominent part. Even when we are alone, sound is a great comfort. It's surprising, for instance, just how many people leave the television switched on, even if they are not watching it. The background noise becomes an ambient sound that is part of our environment. Music or the radio can also be used in the same way. In our household certainly, there's usually a radio on or music playing.

There are so many things to occupy our minds at all times that prayer can seem like an intrusion of spiritual activity into an ordered world of sound and activity. No wonder, when we do get down to prayer, that it is often rushed and hasty, its quality eroded by a multitude of distractions and diversions.

MAKING ROOM FOR GOD

For most of us it's extremely difficult to build into our lives space for God, for creating an atmosphere of worship or prayerfulness that we may find in Christian communities or in monastic orders but seldom in our own homes. The sense of peace, stillness and serenity that we can see in the animal kingdom, however illusory, is something we crave but don't seem to experience. If our prayer life is to be effective and put on firm ground our relationship with God, if we are to know what it is to sense his peace which he offers to us, we must begin with ourselves. There is an inheritance to be claimed: the peace of God. This is not an unobtainable asset available only to the super-spiritual. We do not have to join a monastic order to acquire it. It is the birthright of every Christian.

Whatever tradition we come from within the Christian spectrum, we share with every other Christian the benefits that come from faith in Christ. One of these is the promise of being at peace with God. When God enters a human life he renews it from within, taking away the turmoil and replacing it with his peace, which is of a quality and depth that cannot be imitated. It describes the state of relations between man and God – one of peace, not enmity – but it also describes the experience of God living within.

It is not just a feeling of wellbeing, but a calm sense within that God wants to remain a reality amid all the turmoil. If you have not sensed this for yourself, it is hard to grasp just how concrete an experience this can be. It may sound airy-fairy and something so otherwordly that it cannot be grasped, but in fact it is the very opposite. God's peace has such a solidity and massive density to it that we want to touch it and wrap our hands around it, even though it is God who is wrapping his arms around us. This peace is something within ourselves. It is the springboard for prayer.

INTEGRATING PRAYER INTO LIFE

Many people have an inferiority complex when it comes to their prayer life. They feel a sense of inadequacy because they find it hard to spend the time they feel they should in prayer and when they do find a space, they find themselves filling it up with something else. Reading Christian biographies can sometimes worsen the problem. When I was a student I bought a biography of one of the great men of prayer. He was called 'Praying Hyde', such was his reputation. I read with awe how his 'success rate' (as it seemed to me then) was so high. For this man, answered prayer was a formality. Give him something to pray for and hey presto! there was God just waiting to deliver the answer. Nothing was too much trouble. Here was a man so close to God that every arrow hit the bull's-eye.

The story was meant to inspire, but it had the reverse effect on me, making me all the more aware of my weaknesses. This man was so dedicated in his prayer life, that after he died they found in the floorboards two knee-shaped grooves, worn into the wood by the many hours spent kneeling in prayer. I was stunned and decided not to finish the book. It was too depressing to go on: this man's example was one I could never begin to emulate. He seemed to come through a time warp from a different age altogether, when there was time enough to do the things you set your heart on. But I lived in my own time with its peculiar obsessions and particular pressures. I could admire 'Praying Hyde', but that was it. Relating to him was out of the question. He lived on a different planet from mine. As a role model he was a disaster.

I wonder how many of us actually have role models for prayer with whom we can identify? My closest Christian friend at college was a medical student called Bill, who had the most wonderful singing voice. In fact, he had won his place at the university as a choral scholar and only after he arrived did he switch courses to take up medicine. Bill didn't find the switch to medicine easy. It is one of the most demanding of subjects, combining theoretical knowledge of the human body with all the practical skills that medicine requires. As a member of the college choir he was required to sing in chapel virtually every day and attend regular rehearsals. All of this meant that he had a busy schedule. Yet Bill had two endearing qualities that made all who met him warm to him. He was very gentle by nature and the kind of person who always made time for people. They were drawn to him as a friend with a good listening ear. The second quality he had, which only I, as his close friend, saw, was that he gave priority to prayer. Living in the same house, I quickly discovered how big a part prayer played in his life. Sometimes I would walk into his room in the evening for a coffee and chat, only to find him fast asleep on his knees beside his bed. I was deeply moved by this. Here was a man who took his faith very seriously indeed. Despite the pressure he was under and however tired he was, he set aside much of what little free time he had to pray. Bill was an inspiration to me and showed me by his example the priority that prayer can have in the life of the Christian. He brought my paltry prayer life into perspective.

Prayer is a vital resource in life. Through it we are able to bring to God all our hopes and fears and let him open up a dialogue with us, as we listen and wait. The Psalms make this point far better than I can. These record the richness and colourful tapestry of King David's prayer life, one that was transparently honest and open.

Take Psalm 109. David states his dilemma before God in no uncertain terms – he is feeling badly let down by people he trusted. He feels betrayed. 'Wicked and deceitful men have opened their mouths against me; they have spoken against me with lying tongues . . . In return for my friendship they accuse me, but I am a man of prayer' (Ps. 109: 2, 4). David then moves into a prayer so direct that it takes the breath away. 'May his days be few; may another take his place of leadership . . . May his children be wandering beggars; may they be driven from their ruined homes. May a creditor seize all he has . . .' (Ps. 109: 8–11). He continues to heap upon his enemy every calamity his mind can envisage. It is a prayer of passion and anger, straight from the heart, letting God see for sure the strength of his feelings. The essential point that comes clearly through David's anger is his honesty. He does not try to hide his feelings from God, he is blunt and direct.

I remember how a relatively new Christian in our church was describing some of the turning points in his Christian journey. One of them was an experience of answered prayer that he could barely believe. It was during the year that the Philippines were in turmoil as the dying throes of the Marcos regime and the rising power of Cory Aquino threatened to throw the country into civil war. There were massive demonstrations with the Church at the forefront.

My friend prayed for a bloodless revolution – for Marcos to be deposed and Cory Aquino to take over without any loss of life. It seemed an impossible dream, but he prayed for it with a sincere heart in faith. When it came true he was stunned but thrilled. I'm not saying that, but for this one man's prayers, there would have been a bloody civil war. But I am saying that every prayer is significant and in God's great equation, prayer has a vital part to play in changing our world. My friend's prayer was echoed throughout the world: how good to see it come to pass in what was one of the major international news stories of that year.

FINDING THE TIME

In order to integrate prayer into a busy life it is essential to establish the peace of God I have just outlined and to create space for God in our timetable. This isn't easy and will depend on how good we are at managing our time. More on this in a moment, but first let me tell you two stories.

Norman is in his mid-fifties and commutes to work each day on the London Underground. He is an activist, always busy and rarely still. But when he is commuting to work he has no choice but to sit down on the Central Line for forty-five minutes without deviation, interruption or diversion. What he does is to shut his eyes – not to sleep but to close off his immediate environment and to create space in which to pray. That forty-five minutes of concentrated prayer has become a spiritual lifeline for him. Now I'm not suggesting this arrangement is by any means an ideal one, but it shows how you can find space for God in the most unlikely of circumstances.

Helen is in her thirties. She works in a metropolitan city and commutes into work on British Rail from her home some distance away. Helen is interested in personal growth and development and to this end has started to keep her own spiritual journal. Every morning she looks back at the previous day – not to keep a blow-by-blow record of events

Resources for Confidence

of the day, but to record reflections and observations. Since the journal began she has found that it has become easier to see God's hand at work in her life and in herself. She has been able to work through some ideas. It has clarified her thinking and enabled her to see herself in a new light. An unplanned benefit is that she has found, after a few months of keeping this journal, that she has grown to like herself more, to appreciate herself and not to feel bad about it. It has helped to build her confidence, because the journal has given her life a better perspective. On the canvas of her life, she can now see the whole landscape and not just the detail.

Writing a journal may not sound like prayer as we usually think of it, but it is another way of expressing ourselves before the God whom we are told is so interested in each person that even the hairs on our head are numbered. However busy we may seem to be, it is possible to find ways to integrate prayer into our lives. God is interested in dialogue not monologue: we need to speak and to be silent so that we hear him. It was Elijah who found God, not in thunderous earthquakes, but in a still small voice. Those who are never still will never hear the sounds of silence.

How do you do this? Everyone has their own method. Some pray while gardening: digging the soil is a very humbling task which humankind has performed for thousands of years, and there is time to reflect on the parable of the Sower or on the lost innocence of Eden. A friend of mine leaves a Bible lying around the kitchen. When she sits down for a coffee she picks it up and reads it – a moment snatched for God out of a busy day. Another keeps photographs of friends and missionaries on her fridge door. When she goes to the fridge to get some milk, she prays for the people in the photographs. She also regularly changes them to avoid getting bored or indifferent to them. My wife uses a prie-dieu, a small prayer stool which she keeps beside the bed. One of my habits is to go outside into the garden when locking up the house for the night. I look at the stars, pick out some friendly constellations and inevitably end up praising God for his universe. It clears my mind and focuses my thoughts on God.

Establishing peace and creating space for God then enables us to 'get on with it'. The Texans have a great expression to describe people who are all talk and no action. Such people are 'all hat and no cattle'. Christians who talk about prayer but don't get round to praying are wasting one of their greatest resources. It's like having a Ferrari in your front drive but never going out in it. Looking at it and thinking about it is one thing, but unless you get in the front seat, start the engine, grip the wheel and set off on your journey, the Ferrari is a waste of space. We are not here to mess around on the edges of life but to live it to the full. Spiders don't hang around watching their webs, working out how long it takes a fly to decompose and then constructing a scientific model based on their calculations: they nip in and scoff it!

MUSIC CAN AID PRAYER

Music can be a great aid to prayer, particularly the meditative type when you allow yourself room to think aloud and listen for God. Some of the medieval music available nowadays – Gregorian chant for example – makes a wonderful backdrop for prayer, as do the tapes from the Taizé Community in France. Some of the Taizé music focuses on a single chant which is repeated many times over to aid meditative prayer. I often use the Taizé tape called 'Laudate' in my prayers. When I travel abroad for my job, I take it with me. The chants include 'Stay here and keep watch with me. Watch and pray, watch and pray'. Another moving one is 'Jesus, remember me when you come into your kingdom'. In our local church, the Taizé chant 'O Lord hear my prayer' is often used as a refrain after intercessory prayers.

Music can have a powerful effect on our mood and therefore on the tone of our prayers. The late psychiatrist, Anthony Storr, remarked on Desert Island Discs on Radio 4 that listening to Haydn is of great help to those who feel melancholic and depressed. One of the tapes I have played a lot during the writing of this book is Mahler's Second Symphony in C Minor, 'The Resurrection'. Some people use Christian music to give travelling by car a spiritual dimension. My brother and his family often play tapes of Christian songs and hymns and turn a long journey into a family sing-along. I recently borrowed the use of a car from a church friend called Judy while our vehicle was off the road. When I switched on her cassette player, there was a tape of contemporary Christian music, alongside a Taizé tape. If you like music, it can be a very useful aid to prayer and personal meditation.

THE SLEEP FACTOR

One hundred and fifty scientists and doctors from eight countries met recently at Leicester University to discuss the nature of sleep. Believe it or not, there is still much discussion about the purpose of sleep. One theory is that dreams allow people to exercise parts of the brain not normally used when awake. Another theory is that the mind is clearing out the day's clutter, like a computer erasing old data. Whatever its purpose, sleep is vital for us all.

Without wishing to state the obvious, I have learned from my own experience that if at times I feel low, discouraged and below par, it is almost always because I am physically tired. When we are preoccupied with the day's events or some unsolved problem, getting to sleep can take longer and our mind seems overactive.

When the next day's newspaper is ready to be printed, the front page is finished and the headlines all set, the newspaper is 'put to bed'. It's a good practice to put your mind 'to bed': to put it at rest with God before going to sleep. A time of quiet reading or reflection can help greatly. Some people use the end of day service of Compline to do this, which is broadcast from time to time just before midnight on Radio 4 on Sunday evenings. Within that service is the most superb prayer for the end of the day. I share it with you to encourage you to seek it out and to use it:

> Be present, O merciful Father, through the silent hours of this night, so that we who are wearied by the changes and chances of this fleeting world, may rest in your eternal changelessness, through Jesus Christ our Lord.*

Two or three good nights of sleep can do wonders for your sense of wellbeing. If you want to do an interesting and unusual foray into the Bible, look up what it has to say about sleep. The psalmist says, 'In vain you rise early and stay up late, toiling for food to eat – for he [God] grants sleep to those he loves' (Ps. 127: 2).

Taking time out during the day to relax the mind is also a great restorative. My father-in-law told me a story of the engineers working on the design for the nuclear power station at Hinkley Point in Cornwall. They worked as a team in an office that ran beside a canal. One day, one of the team put his head in his hands, got up from his desk and disappeared. Minutes later he was seen walking along the canal. He did not come back for some time. His colleagues were by now very concerned about him. When he returned he was bombarded with questions. 'What's the matter? Is everything all right?' His reply was terse. 'I'm paid a lot of money to use my brain. My brain was tired, so to give it a rest, I took it for a walk!'

When I was fourteen years of age, my English teacher at school asked everyone in the class to write a short autobiographical essay, describing how we saw ourselves. This essay has somehow survived the passage of time. Part of it describes the curious sleeping habits of Justin Phillips, aged fourteen-and-a-half. The essay prompted a curious comment from my English teacher, who compared my sleeping habits to those of Winston Churchill.

> After a long hard day's work at school, I often sleep for an hour or so after tea, which completely relaxes and

---

* For a version of Compline you can use at home or in groups, I recommend the Grove Worship Series No. 72, *A Late Night Service: Compline in Modern English*, by Mark Davies, Grove Books 1980. This prayer is on p. 18.

rests me both physically and mentally, so I am far better equipped to deal with homework up to any hour. This brief sleep removes the tension and fatigue built up during the day, but I also find I can sleep anywhere, no matter what distractions may be around me.

The English teacher has pencilled in the margin, 'Marvellous idea of Churchill'. I didn't know that then, but Winston Churchill was famous for cat-napping during the day. Looking back, I suspect the truth was that I was so tired after school, I couldn't keep my eyes open. I manage to stay awake more easily nowadays, but curiously in the late afternoon I still find myself feeling lethargic. I come to life again in the late evening, when most people are beginning to flag. This sleep characteristic has undoubtedly influenced my career. No wonder I have spent eight years working on early morning and late night programmes.

I have always seen sleep as a valuable resource and none of us can function as well without it as we can with it. For those who work unusual hours or irregular shifts, cat-napping is sometimes the only way to satisfy the body's need for rest. Another cat-napper is General Norman Schwarzkopf, who commanded the Allied Forces in Operation Desert Storm, the war to recapture Kuwait from Iraq. When he was in London to promote his autobiography, he described his philosophy of sleep.

> Never miss an opportunity to take a nap. That's one of the things I learned in nearly 40 years in the army. In the Gulf War I'd stay up late because the Scuds (Iraqi missiles) usually came in between 2 a.m. and 4 a.m. Then I'd catch maybe two hours sleep before getting up for the morning briefing. And after that I'd take another two or three before Washington woke at three in the afternoon. Over there I also learned to drop off quickly. I had these tapes of nature sounds and they'd relax me, put other things out of my mind. You see, I love the outdoors.*

---

* *Evening Standard*, November 3rd, 1992.

Sleep is a resource than we can adapt to our needs. Politicians are famous for getting by on very little sleep. Journalists travelling with Margaret Thatcher would return with admiration for her stamina and appetite for work, devouring her 'red boxes' of state papers with gusto during the night hours. She could get by with very little sleep. During the Commonwealth Conference in Lusaka at which the future of war-torn Rhodesia was determined and the Lancaster House peace talks set up, the Prime Minister only gave two interviews at the end of the talks. I was one of the two radio journalists summoned to interview her at the end of what had been her first foreign success. She had only been Prime Minister for two months. What was unusual was that she decided to give the interviews at the end of a long, hard day of negotiation, at two o'clock in the morning. And I have to say that she looked a lot fresher and more alert than both of us.

The former Labour Party leader, Neil Kinnock, is the same. He uses both the start and the end of the day for reading and relaxation. As he told the *Radio Times* (October 31st-November 6th, 1992):

> I find I can get a lot done in the quiet hours of the morning, so my day begins at 6.30 a.m. or earlier . . . I always read before I go to sleep unless it's very late. I can manage happily on five hours' sleep a night, but if I go three or four nights with only two, then I'll have a solid seven to catch up. The important thing is not to mess up the next day.

MANAGING YOUR TIME

That other great resource which we fritter away is that of time itself. 'Time and tide wait for no man,' as the English proverb says. In our waking hours, we have the time to do all the things God wants us to do, yet somehow, time has become for many of us the great enemy. Instead of being our servant, time becomes a tyrannical master, robbing us of sleep and stealing away those things we want to do but never quite have the time to do. The fate of the person who abuses and wastes his time was never better explored than by the fiery imagination of Dante Alighieri. 'It is the wisest who grieve most at loss of time,' he wrote.

How can we become better managers of our time? How can we seize control of the great oppressor who, with the passing of the years, seems to make the hands of the clock turn ever faster, until hours appear to become compressed into minutes. We need to lay down some firm guidelines for getting to grips with how we use our time. Let's begin with sorting out our priorities, with what really matters. Taking charge of our schedules can be a great liberating experience and a most useful contributor to our sense of wellbeing and self-confidence.

We cannot replace time. Once gone, it cannot be relived. If we start from the assumption that God gives us all the time we need to do what he requires us to do, then the onus is on us to use that time as best we can. We are stewards of that time. This opens up all sorts of possibilities for us. We can plan how we use our time and have a lot of fun trying to make the best use of it. English cricketer Ian Botham's philosophy of time is that life is not a dress rehearsal: we have our time on earth here and now. It is precious and valuable, so let's use it and try not to waste it. In Jesus's parable of the good steward, it is the one who makes best use of the resources while his master is away who receives the praise and the reward (Luke 19:17). To waste our time is to waste away our life. The hours can slip past more quickly than water runs out of a bath. If you don't put in the plug, it is gone.

How can we, then, plan our time better? The purpose is not to increase the number of things we do, or even the quality of what we are doing, but to ensure that we are making the most of our time. This is not just a question of stewardship alone – using our time to best advantage. I would argue that we can also see it as part of our Christian calling. God has not given us life to treat as a throwaway disposable commodity. It is infinitely valuable and precious. There are ways in which God wants us to use that time, developing our gifts, letting his Spirit work within us, showing his light and sharing with others what we have discovered in his precious gospel. Using our time well is all part of that bigger call to serve our God.

That is a tremendous motivation for us. To please God in our use of time is in itself a driving force that can help us to value our time and not to waste it.

A secular definition of a career is the time taken to achieve our personal, emotional, financial and organisational goals. Inject into that the spiritual momentum of serving God and fulfilling his call for us, and you have a heady recipe. Just think how much each of us could achieve for God if we could only use our portion of time effectively and efficiently.

How much time we have God alone knows. As Ralph W. Sockman put it, 'Time is the deposit each one has in the bank of God and no one knows the balance.'* Time is, first, a gift from God to be used to maximum effect and, for the Christian, for the ultimate glory of God. How we use our time should in itself be a statement of our commitments and priorities. The rich mix of work, leisure and sleep, or whatever goes into our day, should bring us enrichment and fulfilment, physically and spiritually. Time is also our servant and not our master. It is a resource like any other and can be largely under our control. It must, however, be treated with respect and as an opportunity for us. So let's not allow it to be frittered away.

Already we have established two principles to help us plan our time. Time is a gift from God and is, therefore, to be seen as something positive. It is also a resource and subject to us, not master over us. This approach will assist our search for more confidence in who we are and what we do. Just as people make choices as to how they use their money, so we need to plan carefully how we use our time. Busy people need to budget their time. A simple exercise can help – the time pizza.

THE TIME PIZZA

Imagine in your mind a giant, deep-pan pizza. If that pizza represents twenty-four hours of your life, how would you

---

* Tony Castle, *The Hodder Book of Christian Quotations*, Hodder & Stoughton, 1982, p. 241.

divide up the sections proportionally? You may prefer to sketch this on a scrap of paper. One slice could be covered in black olives and represent your sleep. If you are an eight-hour sleeper, then one-third of your pizza has already been served on to your plate as your daily ration of sleep. How do you spend the remaining two-thirds? What proportion of pizza is left to fit in your work, time with your partner and/or family? What about relaxation? Study? Travel? Prayer? Don't forget you must eat as well, so that's another slice gone.

After dividing the pizza into slices of time, check the balance of time that you spend on various activities against the goals and priorities which emerged from the exercises in the first chapter. If you find you are not spending your time on what matters most to you, then it is time to look again. To do this you must make some decisions and some choices. How can you decide what has priority?

URGENT AND IMPORTANT

It is quite extraordinary how we can find the time to do the things we really want to do and yet somehow never quite manage the five minutes or so needed for that awkward, fiddly job. If we can learn to prioritise effectively, we will find our confidence and our self-awareness grow.

Every so often, the U-bend below our kitchen sink gets blocked up with assorted waste and gunge and the joint starts to leak. It's not a serious leak, but the U-bend gently drips foul-smelling water over the cleaning cloths and sprays kept under the sink. My wife's short-term solution is to tie a plastic bag around the pipe to collect the drips. This enables me to put off the job for at least another week. Then the day of reckoning comes.

It's a messy job, requiring the cupboard to be cleared, the bag gingerly to be untied and emptied and the U-bend to be dismantled. It then has to be cleaned out, re-greased and all the washers checked. Not a long job, but one you can't do without getting some odorous gunk on your hands and clothing. How much more pleasant it is to watch television or take the children around the corner to the sweet shop.

I find that a most useful technique to assess the priority I give to the tasks piling up on my conscience like left-over toast is to ask myself two questions. Is it urgent? Is it important? If it is urgent it needs to be done soon. If it is important, it cannot wait too long. If it is important but not urgent, then it can wait until tomorrow. If it is urgent but not important, it should be done this afternoon. If it is urgent and important, then waiting is a luxury I cannot afford: I must do it now! It is a simple but effective formula. It enables me to give the correct priority to tasks.

If, however, the task is neither important nor urgent, it can wait. Indeed, does it need to be done at all? Let's take the payment of household bills as a useful example. A note from the local newsagent asking us to pop in some time to pay our paper bill is neither urgent nor important, although it needs to be done sometime. A bill from our credit card company asking for a payment in three weeks time may be important but it isn't urgent. However, a red invoice from the local electricity board saying our payment is late and threatening to cut off the supply if we don't pay within seven days, now that is demonstrably urgent and important.

Let us imagine that one day our boiler breaks down. It is still producing hot water for the taps, but is not generating enough to heat the radiators. To get it repaired is important, but if this happens in midsummer it is not urgent; it can wait. If, however, this happens in mid-January during the coldest weather with a foot of snow on the ground, we might consider this task both important and urgent!

These two questions – Is it urgent? Is it important? – can cut away the dross and help us determine our priorities. Applying this simple technique will sort out much of the clutter and help us to see our way ahead more clearly. That will enable our confidence to mushroom. Distractions will be reduced and the things that need to be done will get done.

It is a bit like the old philosophy of Watford Football Club: the fast route to goal is the long ball down the middle, no frills, just get the ball in the opposition's penalty area as fast and as often as you can. By the law of averages, you'll win the game.

IDENTIFY THE TIME THIEVES

What are the things that sneak in and rob you of the time you have? These are the activities that may seem fun at the time, but by the end of the day you are saying to yourself: What happened to my day? Why did I get so little done? Here brutal honesty is required, or you will simply kid yourself.

One way to identify the time thieves is to do a time audit on yourself. By writing down every activity and keeping a detailed diary of how you spend your time over a given period, you can discover some of the worst culprits. These are seldom what you expect. Often it is the spontaneous events in life which can eat up your time and over which you have little control. The person who drops by unexpectedly, or the conversation over a half-hour drink that stretches to two hours.

When I was a producer on Radio 4's *Today* programme, the team would breakfast together after the programme. If it had been a particularly good one and team spirit was high, with the adrenalin still pumping away, that breakfast might extend to morning coffee. Occasionally that ran on until lunchtime. I distinctly remember leaving a Chinese restaurant at 4 p.m. and heading off home after a night shift that had actually ended seven hours earlier!

The leaders of our local church once carried out a time audit on our minister to help him find out if he was using his time in the best possible way. We discovered that adequate time for preparation of sermons was being squeezed out by worthwhile but time-consuming pastoral work. He suffered particularly from unscheduled visits during office hours from members of the congregation who wanted his time and his attention. As a result the church went on eventually to appoint a church administrator to help run the minister's diary and protect him from drop-in visitors when he was busy.

I am sure that television is a great gobbler of our time. How often do you plan to spend an evening reading, thinking or talking about some project or task, but instead find yourself transformed into a couch potato? An early evening soap turns into light comedy, then you're watching the news, then a film and suddenly the evening has gone. According to the *UK Media Handbook 1992/1993*, the average British television viewer spends three hours and forty-five minutes tuned in every day – four hours and twenty minutes in winter. The average person sees thirty-three television commercials a day. On top of that the average radio listener spends just under three hours a day listening to the radio and 91 per cent of the UK population switch on during an average week. Radio and television can between them account for up to seven hours a day of the average Briton's time.

Christians are particularly skilled at filling up every available moment with yet another voluntary activity that eats up time faster than a hamster on speed or a lioness with her prey. It is in the nature of churches to offer a variety of activities during the week. In my church we can easily find ourselves attending a church meeting on Monday, a housegroup on Wednesday and helping a youth activity on Friday. If you are a musician in the choir, that takes care of Thursday and suddenly only Tuesday remains. The perfect night on which housegroup leaders can hold their monthly meeting! If our church also lays on family activities such as Barn Dances, then Saturday night is the obvious day. As they say, seven days makes one weak! Whoops, there goes another one. In the words of a friend of mine, today's church is guilty of inflicting on its members the curse of 'hectivism' – hectic activity. What inevitably gets squeezed out is time to think, time to reflect, time to pray and time to be ourselves.

The only way to deal with this is to question what you are doing and why. Again: Is this important? Is it urgent? Do I really need to be there? is a useful liberator.

SAYING 'NO'

A key lesson is learning to say 'no'. A friend of mine called Robert, housemaster at a well-known school, is very good at this. If he is asked to take on some committee or some task that does not fit in with the personal priorities which he believes are right for him, his answer is always 'no'. He is not susceptible to the danger of feeling flattered to be asked, or of being persuaded that he has a special contribution to make. If it doesn't fit in, he will politely but firmly refuse. This in turn frees him up to give time to what he wants to do and to do it well. It's the principle of not spreading ourselves too thinly. We all know that it's only too easy to sacrifice quality for quantity. By doing a great deal we feel something must be achieved. What suffers is the quality of what we are doing.

Have you heard the story of the 'Gourmet Dad'? It was Saturday lunch and time for a snack. The father cooked his daughter a quick cheese on toast. She groaned. 'Not again, Dad! Welsh Rarebit is boring, can't you do better than that?' Spurred into action, her Dad disappeared into the kitchen and emerged five minutes later with the ultimate cheese on toast. His daughter's eyes nearly popped out as she sank her teeth into it. On the toast was spread a thick layer of mango chutney and on top of that was a generous slice of grilled stilton.

'Is that better?' he asked.

'Yummy!' came the reply.

Many of us are in real danger of spreading ourselves so thinly that we dilute the quality of what we do and of who we are. Instead of being the 'fragrance' or 'aroma' of Christ to a world that needs him, to use Paul's graphic description from 2 Corinthians 2: 14–15, our lives give just a 'whiff'. Overcommitment is much like an overdose. Until we learn to prioritise, delegate and say 'no', our confidence and control will suffer. Even if it means being a bit unpopular for a while, it is worth it.

PLANNING OUR TIME

Personal disorganisation is a big time stealer. Organising our time properly and sensibly gains us time. I hope I'm not stating the obvious, but it's worth saying that the first way to run a timetable with more reliability is always to carry a personal diary or organiser. I've lost count of the times a certain friend has forgotten an engagement because she takes great pride in never carrying a diary. She says she can always retain dates in her head. Who is she trying to kid? I use a slimline diary and attach to the inside cover some of those wonderful sticky-back notes that can be used again and again. They act as an instant memo pad to jog my memory.

The second thing is to start writing 'to do' task lists. I use that first ten minutes' quiet of the day or that last five minutes before I go up to bed to write myself a little *aide-memoire* of tomorrow's tasks. I discovered recently that a well-known chain of stationery stores, selling office equipment, cards, pens and envelopes, stocks a pre-printed pad called 'Things to do today!' It consists of forty A5 sheets, each one with twenty numbered lines. The idea is that you write down your list of tasks and tick those that are urgent at the front of the line. When the task is completed you just cross it out or put a second tick at the end of the line to show it's been done.

Whether it's a pre-printed pad or the back of an envelope, all we have to do is to put down essential tasks of the day, such as ringing a friend, paying that bill, writing that 'thank you' letter to a friend, responding to an invitation, ringing the plumber, cancelling that appointment, today's shopping, etc. These are not the kind of things we put in a diary, but are things that might slip out of our mind if we don't remind ourselves to do them.

Thirdly, for larger-scale personal organisation, think about having a family 'to do' board. In our household, with all the demands of a large family, we have a white board stuck on to the back of the door leading into our breakfast room. We can all see it from the table where we eat our cereal in the morning. On the board any of us can write what we like. It might be shopping needs or a prayer request. 'Laura's music exam on Saturday' sits side by side with 'Dangerously low on loo roll'.

Fourthly, we should see if we can find a way of dealing with intrusions. My brother and his family found their evenings were being swallowed up by phone calls. They could never have a meal together as a couple or a family without the phone ringing. It had become a tyrant, yet they felt guilty taking the phone off the hook. Unless you can become ruthless over the phone and tell people you are too busy to talk just now, the answer is to get an answer-phone. Some machines enable you to listen in as messages are being left, so that you can intercept the message and have the conversation then and there, or you can wait for a more convenient moment to return the call. That's what my brother did: the answer-phone was the solution to the problem.

Fifthly, let's try to gain some time that otherwise might be wasted. Travel and waiting times can be transformed and made far more valuable simply by using them to do some reading, writing, thinking or praying. Far better to use that time stuck in a railway carriage usefully than to sit there blowing a fuse and increasing our blood pressure. I carry a small yellow notebook in my pocket to jot down any thoughts I have for later, or to write down 'to do' lists, while I'm sitting on the train. These may vary from household tasks to office jobs or just personal memory joggers. My wife always carries a small sketch pad in her handbag and some pencils, so that if she sees something she wants to sketch, she can do so there and then. Many a painting has started life in this way.

I hesitate to include this, but I fitted a bookshelf at the appropriate height in our lavatory, so that those of our friends who want to take out five minutes to read while otherwise occupied, can do so! Alongside a set of Observer books sits a New Testament.

Sixthly, and very important, we need to plan our leisure time. When we were newlyweds and every evening together was especially precious, my wife and I had a system of planning on a Sunday night which two evenings we would make sure we both kept free for the following week. We stuck little self-adhesive stickers in our diaries on the designated 'free days'. Then if either of us was asked to stay late at work or to go to some activity or other, we could open the diary, point to the spot and say with a clear conscience, 'Sorry – busy that night'. Setting aside evenings to be free at home is essential.

Planning 'free' slots in our schedule for leisure pursuits can make a terrific difference and help enormously to maintain a sense of balance in our life. One of my neighbours is a keen golfer. But as any golfer will tell you, it's not an activity that you can easily fit into a busy schedule. Eighteen holes can take a large number of hours and the nineteenth hole even longer! So he gets up early on a Saturday and meets up with his golfing friends at 6 a.m. so that he can be home by lunchtime. Otherwise his Saturday would have gone altogether.

Sport and physical recreation, as well as being important for our health, are also great ways of working off the stress of the week. They help give us a sense of wellbeing. Sport helps to externalise the tensions which can be so destructive if absorbed internally and suppressed. I wonder how many ulcers could have been averted with some brisk walking, gentle jogging or cycling to the shops.

One week I was feeling under an abnormal amount of pressure at work. I was physically tense, my shoulder muscles were as hard as rock with absorbed tension and I was getting rather short-tempered at home. On the Saturday morning I put on my tracksuit and trainers and went for a brisk walk and then a jog along the Grand Union Canal close to where I live. I ran off the tension and God rewarded me with the sight of two kingfishers flying along the canal. It is hard to believe, I know, but the kingfishers were within one hundred metres of the A4, the road to Heathrow Airport! I am not really a sporty type, much as I love watching sport, but brisk walking and gentle jogging does seem to suit me and I've now built this into my routine, aiming to get out for an hour or so every week. Of course, the more exercise you get, the more beneficial it can be. Sometimes I listen to music on my personal stereo as I run. At other times I use the time to pray, an oasis in life's dry places.

The confident person is someone who has learned how to handle pressure and to deal with anxiety. That is not to say that worry is eliminated – far from it – but it finds its proper place in a wider perspective. The Olympic athlete Michael Johnson was a hot favourite to win the 200 metres Gold Medal at Barcelona, but he failed to make the final. He was disappointed, certainly, but he reminded reporters that it was only a race and that when he woke up in the morning the sun would still be shining. A losing Wimbledon finalist said afterwards: 'It's only tennis – no one has died'.

PERSONAL ANXIETY

Keeping that sense of perspective can be very difficult indeed. If our life is falling apart around our ears, the person who says, 'Chin up – it could be worse,' is liable to end up with their chin walking into a fist! The instant comforter can prove to be a very insensitive friend. In my view, the most sensible advice ever given to the anxious was delivered by Jesus Christ in the Sermon on the Mount. In our angst-ridden generation, Jesus urges us to keep a proper sense of proportion – to remember just how well God our Father does look after our basic needs.

Anxiety is a topic on which Jesus had much to say: hardly surprising when you think what obstacles Jesus had to overcome to fulfil his own mission. He was not just up against the scepticism of his own family (bar Mary) and the opposition of religious leaders of his day, but also the slowness of his chosen band of followers to grasp the truth of his ministry. The fact that their Master was to suffer and die and rise again was, not surprisingly, very hard for Jesus's disciples to get their minds around. At the very end, Jesus himself had to overcome his own inner turmoil and doubts and surrender his will afresh in the Garden of Gethsemane.

Jesus is direct and leaves no uncertainty about what he is saying. We have a choice to make. No one can serve two masters: you cannot serve both God and money. Once that choice is made, Jesus says, 'Do not worry about your life, what you will eat or drink; or about your body, what you will wear' (Matt. 6: 25a). It's a matter of priorities. 'Is not life more important than food, and the body more important than clothes?' (6: 25b) Having told us to see how God looks after the birds, Jesus reminds us that we are more valuable than they. 'Who of you by worrying can add a single hour to his life?' (6: 27) No, God knows our needs and will supply them. Our task is rather to give priority to getting to know Jesus and his teaching better – in the biblical phrase, to 'seek first his kingdom and his righteousness' (6: 33), and all these things shall be given to us. 'Therefore,' Jesus concludes, 'do not worry about tomorrow, for tomorrow will worry about itself. Each day has enough trouble of its own' (6: 34). That is easy enough to say, but much harder to do. All of us can be worriers at times. Sometimes there seems a lot to worry about.

Peter is almost forty and is married with four children. He works in a highly specialised area of the electronics industry. The company he worked for was swallowed up in a merger and within a couple of years he found himself looking redundancy in the face. This has been the experience of many thousands as the nation's recession bites hard into our lives. Peter had more reason than most to worry. He had moved house with his family out of London to be close to the company's offices in the middle of nowhere, only to find that the company was falling victim to a takeover and cuts. He and his family prayed hard about what to do. Instead of seeking a new job, Peter took the brave step of setting himself up in business, offering his specialised skills to the marketplace. He's making a good go of it and that confidence backed by prayer has reaped its own rewards.

With three million people without jobs in the United Kingdom, the old concepts of job security and of staying in the same job for much of our life have long since gone by the board. A great deal has been written about the long-term effects of unemployment and the demoralising effect it can have on individuals and families. The loss of self-respect and self-esteem can be devastating. None of us should underestimate the real pain and anxiety that unemployment can bring. For the long-term unemployed, it can be especially devastating. It would be foolish of me to pretend that anxiety on this scale can be swept aside by a single prayer or by a change of attitude. Of course it can't. But I do believe passionately that God can enter our situation and share our pain.

Sue is an actress and the realities of her profession are that at any one time, 80 to 90 per cent of actors and actresses are out of work. In Sue's profession, insecurity is a way of life. It goes with the territory. When she has work, she is grateful and enjoys it. When she doesn't, it can be a struggle to maintain her confidence. Her ability as an actress remains unchanged, but she just happens not to be working. It's not easy, but she copes. The worry of where the next job will come from does not go away, but the support of her friends and her local church fellowship can go a long way to keep her buoyant and hopeful.

In this chapter I have tried to address some of the essential ingredients that can help us take more control of our lives and so live in greater confidence. We have talked about integrating prayer into our schedules, about the importance of sleep, about managing time and starting to deal with personal anxiety. I want to end with a case study in confident living based on one of those Old Testament heroes who was anything but a spiritual giant. His name was Gideon, more of a Buster Keaton than an Arnold Schwarzenegger figure.

GIDEON'S CASE STUDY

Gideon is a brilliant case study in confidence – or rather the lack of it. He was the kind of man who would never buy a second-hand car. Gideon would need to meet the manufacturer in person, receive the warranty and have a year's free driving before he'd unlock his wallet. You can tell that by the fact that it is Gideon who puts God to the test, not the other way around. Normally it is God testing us, but not with Gideon. He wants his fleece dry on a wet night and wet on a dry night. I'm surprised he didn't ask for added whitener at the same time.

It is much easier for us to identify with a Gideon than with a Moses or Abraham. With the passage of the years and the help of Hollywood, the founding fathers of Israel still appear to us as spiritual giants. Those who have seen Charlton Heston straddling the Red Sea in *The Ten Commandments* find the image compelling. But Gideon is another matter altogether.

He is somehow far more like us. He's a much more sheepish figure, needing constant reassurance and encouragement and not prepared to take anything at face value. Yet by any standards, Gideon comes through as a high achiever.

His story can be found in the sixth chapter of the book of Judges. The situation is straight out of Hollywood. The Midianites (in the black hats) have taken over the valley. The Israelites (in the white hats) who should be there are hiding in caves and mountains. The Israelites are paying the penalty for abandoning the God who had proved himself for a local fly-by-night god of the locality. Gideon makes his first appearance threshing wheat in a winepress – a bit of subversive activity to deceive the Midianites. God's messenger appears to Gideon and calls him a 'mighty warrior' (Judg. 6: 12). But a Terminator Gideon is not.

'If the LORD is with us, why has all this happened to us?' (6: 13) replies the hapless youth. God's reply gives us our first principle from Gideon's story.

'Go in the strength you have and save Israel' (6: 14). That's a good text to hang on to. Gideon does not reply, 'Just watch me go!' What he does is to put in a request for sick leave.

'How can I save Israel? My clan is the weakest . . . and I am the least in my family'(6: 15). Here comes the second principle we can use for ourselves.

'I will be with you' (6: 16). We are not alone. God tells Gideon he will strike down the Midianites. Gideon then seeks his money-back guarantee and makes an offering that is consumed by fire from a rock. Gideon is at last at peace and is told he will not die. He is told to tear down his own father's altar to the false god called Baal. How does our hero tackle this? He sneaks out at night and does it under cover of darkness because he is afraid of his family and the local gangs. Timid it may be, but the point is that Gideon does not shirk the task. Unfortunately the trick fails, Gideon is identified as the vandal and soon they are baying for his blood. Gideon defies his enemies and challenges them. Here we see the third key to Gideon's success.

'The Spirit of the LORD came upon Gideon, and he blew a trumpet' (6: 34), summoning his supporters. God will give us

the resources we need to do the job he wants us to do. Only at this stage in the story does Gideon again seek reassurance from God by laying down a fleece on the threshing-floor. The dew fell only on the fleece, leaving the ground dry. The next night it was the other way around. But Gideon's army is far too big for the task in hand, says the Lord. So the numbers are pruned, first by voluntary redundancy, and then by a selection exam in which those who cup hands to drink from spring water are chosen but those who lap the water like dogs are booted out. One dream later, Gideon's band of 300 drinkers of mineral water, armed with trumpets and empty jars with torches inside them, scare the living daylights out of the Midianite hordes by blowing their trumpets and smashing the jars in the dark. Panic does the rest. The men in the camps turn on each other with their swords and the rest run away. Gideon has succeeded.

Those three principles are good to have in mind in our search for a more confident expression of ourselves and our faith. God wants to use us as we are: his acceptance of each of us in Christ is fundamental to the gospel. Even our low calibre raw material is enough for God to work wonders with in the world. Like Gideon we should 'go in the strength we have' with a bold front. We can afford to be upbeat because we do not go alone. We are with God and he will equip us with the resources we need to live the life he wants and to accomplish whatever tasks lie ahead.

The example of Gideon is an inspiration to us. The potential is there for God to tap – if we are available and willing and go forward in a positive, 'can do' frame of mind, there is no limit to what can be achieved. If our natural tendency is to be cautious and to hold back, God understands that. But if we can capture for ourselves Gideon's sense of adventure despite all his hesitations, then the Midianites in our life can stand back and tremble. In Saint Paul's equation: 'We live by faith, not by sight. We are confident . . . So we make it our goal to please him' (2 Cor. 5: 7–9).

Jesus presents an invitation to every person that only the most churlish or foolish could refuse. In an age when anxiety has become a growth industry, its appeal is direct and breathtaking in its simplicity. To all of us who carry burdens we cannot bear and who are worriers, Jesus says this: 'Come to me, all you who are weary and burdened, and I will give you rest' (Matt. 11: 28). Using a picture taken from the farming world where cattle would carry a yoke, he says, 'Take my yoke upon you and learn from me, for I am gentle and humble in heart, and you will find rest for your souls. For my yoke is easy and my burden is light' (11: 29–30). Those are words that liberate us. That set us free. It means that Jesus is ready and willing to lift the burdens from our sagging shoulders and carry them himself.

If we have difficulty letting go of our anxieties, here is a simple exercise that can help us. Imagine packing all the anxieties into a cardboard box. Seal the lid, wrap it up in gift paper, put a bow on the top and hand it over in prayer to God. Let him take away the box, and with it the worries. They are now in God's domain and we are free of them.

In that sense we are a mirror. Our lives should reflect what God is doing in our lives. Jesus put it like this in the Sermon on the Mount: 'Let your light shine before men, that they may see your good deeds and praise your Father in heaven' (Matt. 5: 16).

5
CONFIDENCE IN THE FUTURE

There are two hedgehogs in our back garden. I know because I have heard them and seen them foraging for food in the early hours of the morning. Hedgehogs are highly efficient gardeners. In return for the use of my garden, they repay me by eating every snail and slug in sight. I can grow lettuces and other vegetables without worrying about slugs because my hedgehog friends will eradicate them for me. They also seem to be more intelligent than some of their compatriots. As autumn turns into winter, they build up the fat in their bodies and seek out a quiet corner to rest for the winter. They resist the temptation to sleep in our pile of debris for the bonfire, which is a popular hedgehog thing to do, with disastrous results on Guy Fawke's night. Instead they've found a quiet niche under my neighbour's tool shed. Come the winter, their bodies are plump with snails and slugs and they can hibernate in confidence. Hedgehogs are good life planners and much to be admired.

Like the hedgehog, we can also become confident in our future. It is possible to take a long, strategic look at our lives and to make whatever changes we wish in order to bring forward those things we want to do. Of course, the unexpected will always come along and is capable of changing our direction or throwing us off course, but, with God's grace, we can plan for the future. It's perfectly possible to introduce changes that can make all the difference to our sense of purpose and help us to find new direction. One of the mose beautiful affirmations of life planning is to be found in Psalm 121.

'I lift up my eyes to the hills – where does my help come from? My help comes from the LORD, the Maker of heaven and earth . . . The LORD will keep you from all harm – he will watch over your life; the LORD will watch over your coming and going both now and for evermore' (Ps. 121: 1–2, 7–8). Now coming from King David who had more narrow escapes than Houdini, that is a powerful statement of confident faith in the future. He looked to God and so can we. He lifted his eyes from his immediate predicament and looked ahead to the future, knowing God was there to watch over him. So it is with us.

To find that confidence in our life planning, short-term goals are not going to be sufficient. When Norman Lamont resigned as British Chancellor of the Exchequer, in his resignation speech to the House of Commons he made a savage attack on the Conservative Government he had just left. Rightly or wrongly, he accused his former Cabinet colleagues of short-termism, of being in office but not in power, of being swept along by events. If that can be true of governments, it can most certainly be true of us as individuals. There are times when we might feel that we, too, are being carried along in the stream, swept forward by events over which we seem to have little control. Like a plastic duck in a bathtub, we can find ourselves tossed around by the ripples of life. But it doesn't have to be like that. It is perfectly possible to plan for the future and to set our eyes on some future goal. To reach it may mean that we need to make changes in how we live, but over the longer term all is possible.

As Christians we can be confident in our future. Few people in history have experienced such a degree of personal suffering and hardship as the apostle Paul, yet he was able to tell the church of Philippi: 'In all my prayers for all of you, I always pray with joy because of your partnership in the gospel from the first day until now, being confident of this, that he who began a good work in you will carry it on to completion until the day of Christ Jesus' (Phil. 1: 4–6). What is true for the Christian believer in Philippi is no less true for you and me; and that can encourage us as we start our life planning.

We shall begin with where we are now and who we are. To do this requires an honest assessment of our needs and our capabilities – easier for hedgehogs than for humans! For us, getting to know who we are is one of the most important and challenging tasks we may face.

HONESTY HAS A PRICE TAG

There is a distinction to be made between honesty (seeing both the good and the bad) and looking only for the good. The danger is self-delusion. Sometimes there is a price to be paid for being honest. Last year I was invited to speak at the evening service of a popular Anglican church. It has a large congregation and they came along to hear me talk about the media in modern society. I had a choice to make. I could tell them what I thought they wanted to hear, or I could be frank and give them my own views, which may be rather different. Most Christians have strong views on the media and I know that many fear its influence and have justified concerns about issues such as violence and exploitation. Quite a number of Christians see the media as a damaging and corrupt influence with too much power for its own good. They see it as a God-forsaken arena in which any committed Christian should work with fear and trembling. This is an exaggeration, I know, but it is still a view held by some. I sensed this is what they expected to hear from me. It's not a view I share, so I was afraid that by speaking with honesty, I would risk upsetting some of the congregation.

Although I knew that by portraying the media in a positive light, seeing it as an opportunity for Christians to do good work from a Christian perspective and to bring Christian values into their workplace, I might upset some people, I was frank and honest and spoke in positive and glowing terms about the potential of the media and the opportunities for Christians working within it. I talked about it as part of God's creation and therefore made ultimately – like everything else – to glorify him. I also showed how popular television is often reflecting society as much as shaping it, showing us what we are like, even if we don't like what we see. As I feared, the response was at times quite hostile. By offering an alternative to the stereotype negative view that some Christians have, I had clearly touched a raw nerve.

However, I had no doubt that I had done the right thing. I had been open and honest about myself, even if it wasn't what they had come to hear. What happened that night did upset me and knock my confidence a little. It was a talk I had given many times before, but usually to fellow professionals within the media who understand how the media works. To encounter a hostile reaction from fellow Christians was undermining and made me rather angry. But honesty and truth have a price that can't be shirked.

Honesty is very important to building personal confidence. If we are not honest with ourselves, we will not be honest with others. To pretend we are something we are not is dishonest and dangerous. This path has its own penalty built into it. Like the swimmer anxious to show off to his friends how cool he is in television soaps such as *Baywatch* or *Home and Away*, we may be tempted to go into the water out of our depth. Instead of being in control, we find ourselves in need of rescue. There aren't always lifeguards on the beaches of our lives, but there is our faith in the true and living God. He can provide the necessary direction and purpose to keep our feet firmly on the ground. The confident Christian knows where he or she is weak and needs help.

Not knowing what we are really like also puts obstacles in our path that can send us off on the wrong course and slow down that vital process of personal growth that will make us 'me'. The New Testament links good decision making (i.e. knowing what is pleasing to God) to personal and spiritual development. Paul's conditions for being able to 'test and approve' God's way for us is for us to offer ourselves to God wholly and to be transformed by the renewal of our minds (Rom. 12: 1–2). This he sets out as a clear alternative strategy to meekly trying to conform to wordly and secular patterns. This double process of 'offering' and 'transforming' he describes in spiritual terms as an act of worship.

Secular books see 'knowing yourself' as a protection policy against making ill-judged decisions, particularly in career terms. Perish the thought that a person should

Confidence in the Future

find themselves in a difficult situation from which they cannot extricate themselves because they do not know themselves.

I knew a young, talented broadcaster who was given a six-month assignment as a programme producer. His name was Neil and he was in his mid-twenties – a pleasant, easy-going personality who looked as if he would cope well. He happened to be assigned to a fast-moving live programme. He had good ideas, useful contacts and was able to arrange interviews without difficulty. Where he came unstuck, however, was the other side of the job, the instant decision making needed in the studio. This requires a mastery of the stopwatch and agile mental arithmetic in units of sixty to add up seconds into minutes, instantly.

The problem with Neil was that he was mildly dyslexic and nobody knew this. He had trouble reading the studio clock and could not add up timings quickly. As a result he was never in control in the studio and that undermined his confidence and unnerved the programme presenter. He was in the wrong job, a square peg in a round hole. So Neil changed direction and became a reporter and presenter. In this he has been very successful – a round peg in a round hole. But he needed to go through the painful experience of failure in the studio to discover that. He was getting to know himself.

When she went on *Desert Island Discs* on Radio 4, singer Joan Armatrading was asked the stock question about how she'd cope with total isolation. 'When can I go?' she said. She is a quiet and self-sufficient lady and can happily go for weeks without seeing a soul. 'I never wanted to be part of a gang, I just never liked people.' On stage she exudes confidence but she is no extrovert; the reverse in fact. 'I was painfully shy and didn't have any special friends at school,' she told a reporter, 'but it never really bothered me. I was very happy just being in the playground and watching everyone else play.' She's a self-confessed loner who's never been lonely. She knows herself and has used that unusual quality in her music. 'I've always been on the outside watching. That's why my songs are observation songs.' She has no problems with her self-esteem. 'I don't take any notice of what other people think of me, this is me and that's it.' Here is someone who seems to know who she is.

THE DANGERS OF STEREOTYPING

People are infinitely complex and complicated. That's bound to be the case – after all, we are made in the image of God. It's a great mistake to try to categorise people into watertight compartments. It's a cop-out to reduce people to being either introvert or extrovert. How rapidly we pigeonhole people – he's shy, she's really confident, he's only interested in himself, and so on. Some of our greatest dramatic talents, for example Sir Alec Guinness, shy away from publicity and attention. Other great attention seekers can also be capable of acts of sensitivity and kindness.

We do not need to conform to any particular personality or stereotype. It is foolish for extroverts to want to be transformed into introverts, or for introverts to want to become extrovert. That would be to go against the grain of our natures. What makes an antique wooden table so beautiful is the grain in the wood overlaid through the passage of time by that mysterious quality of antiques called the 'patina'. Reproduction furniture tries to mimic this with artificial aging and a few bangs of a hammer, but you cannot fool the eye. The charm of beautiful furniture is the craftsmanship and the finished appearance. The 'patina' in our lives is the combination of all those moments when we have been stretched, when we have suffered, when we have laughed, when we have been truly 'alive'.

A solid oak Victorian kitchen table will carry on its surface all the marks and scratches and knife marks of generations of families who have used it for eating, working and playing games. Those knife marks don't detract from its value: they add to its charm and testify to its life. The face of a North Sea fisherman may be weatherbeaten and lined, showing someone who has confronted the elements and withstood the wind and the storms. Every face tells its own story. It is unique.

For each of us, those experiences that have made us what we are may include much suffering and pain. These are not to be dismissed or suppressed. Even personal pain has value to us. Anyone who has suffered bereavement or struggled with illness knows what a test it can be and how it can bring out depths in our character and make-up, and resilience of which we may have had little knowledge before. That is not to say that pain is good or desirable, but it can deepen us and be of value to us. It becomes part of the 'patina' of our life.

In saying that we should be ourselves and avoid stereotypes, I am not arguing that an inward-looking person cannot become more outward-going and overcome the drawbacks of shyness. In the same way many extroverts would benefit by learning to be more sensitive to others and by learning to listen more carefully. What matters is to aim to become the person God really wants us to be – to be freed to be truly ourselves. This is what that terribly pious and misleading word 'sanctification' means. It is a process of healthy change towards what God wants us to be, which means reflecting more and more of his character – the image, in fact, of Jesus Christ. It is not a process of sanitising who we are, making us sterile as personalities.

There is a brilliant, if frightening, science fiction film called *Invasion of the Body Snatchers*. In the plot, plant spores arrive on Earth from outer space and start to breed unnoticed on our planet. What they hatch are invisible alien life forms that take up residence in human bodies. People are replaced by inert duplicates hatched from alien 'pods'. The replica humans have no emotions, no inner life: they are like robots. Some people worry that to have deep Christian convictions might turn us into Identikit people with no personality. In fact the opposite is true. Christians may share common values and beliefs, but at the heart of our faith is God enabling us to be truly ourselves, enhancing us, not diminishing us.

The outside reflects the inside. As our 'patina' develops with the character forming and special moments of our life, so within us God is at work renewing us. He wants each of us to be the fulfilled, rounded and balanced person he always intended us to be, to be more and more like Jesus

Christ himself. To describe this the New Testament talks about the work of the Spirit of God within our hearts and minds. Significantly the verbs used are always those of gentle and gradual change – words such as guide, lead, mould and renew. The image is that of a potter moulding the clay into a beautiful pot. It is the language of loving and creative care. We do not have a God who bashes us into shape or beats us into pulp to rebuild us. We are not divine Meccano sets or concrete waiting to be reinforced with steel girders. 'We have this treasure in jars of clay to show that this all-surpassing power is from God and not from us,' writes the apostle Paul in 2 Corinthians 4: 7.

Remember that if we take Jesus as our example we are not dealing with a man who wore robes of state and spoke from a pulpit ten feet above contradiction. Jesus was a man of the people. We are dealing with someone who chose prostitutes and publicans to be amongst his circle of friends. Jesus thrived on being with what was seen then as 'bad company'. Moreover, he had the courage to build his church on the dubious characters he mingled with! So in building confidence in who we are, we must first of all accept who we are.

THE SIMON PETER PRINCIPLE

Letting your real personality come through and being your true self does not happen quickly. The example of Simon Peter underlines the principle. One of those dubious friends of Jesus was the Galilean fisherman introduced by his brother Andrew. When Jesus turned Simon the fisherman into Peter the apostle it wasn't something that happened quickly or suddenly. It was a long and, at times, painful process. Simon Peter's character had many rough edges to be smoothed off. He had a short fuse, as one poor lad discovered when Jesus was taken prisoner in the Garden of Gethsemane. Peter was quick to pull out his sword and take a lunge at the high priest's servant, severing his ear.

Yet it was in this rough-hewn fisherman that Jesus found

Confidence in the Future

the person on whom he was to build his church. To Peter fell the task of persuading the Jews of his day of Jesus's true identity as the Messiah. To Paul fell the task of taking the Jesus story into the world beyond Judaism and ultimately to you and me.

In Peter's earlier life we see how Jesus used Peter's failures to turn them into lessons from which he would learn. We learn more from our failures than from any number of successes. There were distressingly painful episodes that could so easily have broken a lesser man, such as his denial of Christ three times over. Sometimes Peter probably found himself embarrassed by Jesus's unpredictable behaviour. An example is the Last Supper when it was Judas, not Peter, who sat beside Jesus in the place of honour. The same night Peter felt very uncomfortable with Jesus washing his feet.

It takes time to change and in Peter's case, the process continued after Jesus's death and resurrection. Remember how reluctant Peter was to visit the house of the non-Jew Cornelius in Caesarea? He had to overcome a lifetime's practice to accept that the non-Jew was included in God's purposes and that what he, as a Jew, had always considered unclean was now acceptable. They didn't have pork scratchings in Peter's day, but if they had, no self-respecting first-century Jew would order them with their pub pint!

Peter was stubborn. Being slow to grasp the universal nature of the Christian faith, he stuck to Jewish rituals on matters such as food when it was no longer obligatory in the new freedom Jesus gives. Paul refers to an argument with Peter over this in his letter to the Galatians. 'I opposed him to his face, because he was clearly in the wrong,' says Paul with confidence: no wimp he· (Gal. 2: 11).

Yet it was Peter who was the first of the disciples to recognise Jesus's true identity as the Messiah (Mark 8: 27–30). This is a turning-point in the gospel accounts. It also turned Peter around. Sure, he was to go on to make many mistakes. His impetuous nature would always land him in trouble. But Peter's heart was in the right place – his loyalty to Jesus was to survive many tests. From this rough man of the sea, Jesus found his rock-hard diamond, the cutting edge of the Church.

What we want to aim for in getting to know ourselves is to discover what we are really like, to fulfil what God wants to do in our lives. We are not likely to be called to be a Peter or Paul, to change the world for ever. In his attempt to define 'the normal Christian life', the Chinese Christian leader Watchman Nee came to the conclusion that the Christian life is something very different from the life of the average Christian. It is defined by Paul in Galatians 2: 20 as 'no longer I but Christ'. Nee argues that the normal Christian life is to let Christ live his life in and through us. That way we will discover what we are really like.

As we move on towards a practical exercise, we have established some first principles. It is important to be honest about ourselves and to resist any temptation to pretend or to imagine we are more than we really are. Honesty in self-appraisal is the aim. We have also seen, from the story of Peter, that we can change and that when God works within us, he is making us more truly ourselves. We are not trying to become like an Identikit Christian – a ghastly prospect! If we wonder whether we can make the change and improve our life, the answer is that we can. God is able to transform us utterly and to bring out all those qualities and characteristics that are dormant or latent within us. He wants us to live fulfilled and purposeful lives. This is living in full colour not in black and white.

It is time to get down to the key exercise in this chapter to help us get to know ourselves better. Let me say at this point that all exercises suggested in this book are just that – suggested exercises and no more. They are aids to understanding, signposts along the route. You should not in any way over-emphasise their significance or attach too much importance to them. In getting to know yourself, these are just simple tools which can help you to unlock a few doors within yourself. Living as we do in an era when we are overwhelmed with psycho-babble and 'new age' thinking, I am anxious not to mislead you or to fall into that trap. These are well-tried and simple methods of

Confidence in the Future 105

looking at yourself in a fresh way. It involves asking some basic questions.

You may find it helpful to have paper and pencil at hand to jot down ideas that come to mind as you read. If you keep a spiritual diary you will want to reflect on what you are about to read. Or just read on and think it over at your leisure.

THE TIME TRAVEL EXERCISE

The purpose of this exercise is to increase our personal confidence by giving us a clearer sense of our own identity and personality. By going through the process of some honest self-appraisal, we will be better equipped to face the future and whatever it holds for us. Confidence comes from within, so to be a confident Christian it will help us to have a firm idea of what we are really like and of who we are.

We will begin by looking at the ingredients that have made us what we are today. Like Dr Who in his time travelling police telephone box, the Tardis, we're going to travel back in time to look at our past, at our roots. Then we will take a rigorous look at our present situation and ask some penetrating questions. We are then in a position to look ahead to the future and set some personal targets. From this exercise some things will become much clearer and we will begin to feel more in control of our lives. All this is a part of building up our personal confidence.

In a sense we are attempting to cut through the undergrowth to let some raw light into the dark areas of our lives. Just as the high canopy enables the rich life of the tropical forest to flourish, so we are going to project ourselves above the forest floor of our lives to let some light into our growth areas. Let's begin with our gnarled and knotted roots.

THE TIME ZONES

These are the three time zones to think through. Next to each zone I have put the key question or questions we are to address in the following pages. For those who like visual imagery, I have also suggested a picture, an image to assist your imagination to unlock the doors of your mind. Remember that that answering these questions will help our personal confidence. We will know who we are and learn to live with ourselves more easily.

- **The past** How did I get here? (Past influences)
  Image: What has given us our 'patina' or make-up?
- **The present** Who am I? (How we see ourselves)
  Image: Our 'internal community', or aspects of our personality.
- **The future** Where am I heading? (Goals and direction)
  Anything in the way? (Hurdles and hazards)
  What do I need? (Resources)
  Image: What traffic blocks our way?

This journey of self-discovery is not intended to be a solo voyage across the universe. Try to bring God into the process. Sit quietly in a relaxed position, breathe deeply, releasing any tension and, if you feel able, quietly ask God to open some doors in your thinking as you read on. As you go through the next few pages, notice any words or feelings, any mental pictures or thoughts that come to mind as you focus on each question. If you feel like it, write down in words or sketch in a drawing or diagram what comes into your mind. Don't dwell overlong on any single thought – see what floats to the surface.

THE PAST: HOW DID I GET HERE?

This is a question that deals with your roots and the influences on your life. For all of us our upbringing is a central influence. When Anthony Clare sits 'In the Psychiatrist's Chair' on BBC Radio 4, invariably his guests discuss the influence their respective parents have played in their lives. Our value systems will derive as much from our home as from anything else.

Don't be judgmental here – it's not helpful to start laying blame or giving credit at this stage for your strengths or your shortcomings. I'm really asking you to think about your values and where they come from. Home, school and religious backgrounds come into play here. There will no doubt be particular relations or friends, too.

To help you in this task, let me briefly identify some of those influences in my own life. It is easy to identify how different traits I have today derive directly from some of the influences of my childhood. My desire to do well at school and go on to university came from my father, who was ambitious for me to succeed where he himself had experienced frustration. For family reasons, he had left Oxford University without completing his degree.

My mother always encouraged her children's eccentricities and gave us a strong sense of self-identity. She encouraged us in our interests and gave us plenty of freedom in how we dressed and what we looked like. Though she had to bring up five children with a wide span of ages – there were seventeen years between oldest and youngest – each of us is our own person, quite unlike the others. The other big childhood influence in my life was my Uncle Humphrey, who spent his whole career teaching mathematics in one Norfolk grammar school. He introduced me to the charm of cricket, the mysteries of the universe through astronomy, the fun of collecting fossils. He also took me on an art tour of Italy. So it is that cricket, astronomy, art and fossils remain high on my list of interests to this day.

The Christian influence of my upbringing gave me a positive and supportive context in which to make my own decisions about the spiritual dimension to my life. The direction of my life was shaped by my upbringing in a Christian family in an atmosphere where each of us was left to our own devices in working out our priorities in life. I never felt under any parental pressure in working out where I stood or what I believed. I was brought up as a regular churchgoer, but no pressure was put on me if I decided not to go. As a boy I went along with my brother to a Crusaders Bible class and there I learned my way around the Bible and made friendships which have lasted all my life. I took along many of my school friends – two of whom are now Anglican clergymen!

All of this came together in one of those life-changing moments. I became a Christian in France on a house party in Brittany for schoolboys. The holiday leader, a businessman called Tony Gill, spoke to us about his life and of the need to make a commitment to Jesus Christ, to enable him to pilot us safely through the choppy waters of life. That was when I became a Christian and handed my past, present and future into God's safe hands with a simple prayer of whispered confession and commitment. I can still recall the deep sense of innermost joy. I remember laughing with delight. I don't know what my roommate must have thought at the time!

SPIRITUAL ROOTS

It does our confidence good to remember the path we have trodden in our personal journey with God. Though some people become Christians in an instant from apparently no spiritual background at all, for most of us it is a more gradual process. Like John Bunyan's pilgrim, Christian, we have been on a journey with God. Looking back, sometimes we can see his footprints alongside ours. At other times he has carried us over periods of doubt and hard days and we see only one set of footprints. Tracing our spiritual roots reaffirms our Christian identity and feeds our confidence, like a plant sucking up nitrogen.

What are your spiritual roots? If you are reading this as a Christian, how did you get where you are now? Was it the friendship of an individual, the prayers of a relation, the upbringing at home or perhaps a personal quest for God? Maybe it was a book you read, or the example of a Christian friend. Perhaps it was all those years of going to church. Or was it what seemed at the time to be a chance encounter? At our local church in West London, we have had people just walk in for no apparent reason off the street: they were passing by and were curious to see what went on in church on a Sunday morning.

How did you come to faith? Was it at a specific time in your life or gradually over a period of time? Some Christians can tell you the minute and the hour of the day when God came into their lives. Many Christians cannot remember any specific moment; it was a gradual coming to faith over a period of time. But every Christian should be able to sense the roots of his or her faith. Look at how a plant grows in the garden. Without the right soil, moisture from the rain and heat from the sun to let the seed germinate, it would not be there. We should be able to identify, or at least recall, the seedbed of our faith.

If you are agnostic or atheist, the question still applies: what brought you to this position of unbelief? Does the Christian faith just seem too incredible to be true, a fallacy based on a fantasy? Perhaps a strong influence in your life told you that you are alone in this world and that there is no God. Or perhaps you have been through some personal ordeal that has crushed what faith you had, so that God seems a mirage or an illusion. Or is it simply that you have never thought about it?

The question is, how do we see the hand of God in our life? Looking at these influences can help to sharpen the focus on where we are now. Do you feel supported by your past, or have you broken away from it? Do you see the continuity, or is there a conscious breaking away at some point? What influences remain in your life? Where have you tacked your own course? Are there particular events, as well as people, that proved to be of great significance? Maybe, to use an extremely unlikely example, you went to see the Moscow State Circus as a child and determined to become a lion tamer! Or maybe a grandparent was a role model for you and you decided to follow their example in your career? It's surprising how many people in the armed forces or in the police come from a forces or police background. It's true in broadcasting, too. You don't have to look very far to see sons and daughters of broadcasters following where their parents have gone before. In the acting profession the Redgrave family has become a huge dynasty of acting talents, just as the Fonda family have in the United States.

Knowing our personal roots helps us to understand where we have come from and how we got to where we are today. It gives us a context and a platform for our lives. A sprinter needs a set of blocks in which to place his feet to give him a firm start. A trampolinist needs a trampoline if he is to somersault ten feet in the air. A research scientist needs to have studied her topic for many years if she is to discover a cure for cancer or for AIDS. None of us can go forward and achieve our future without a firm foundation. Knowing our spiritual roots will make all the difference. It gives us confidence. Knowing God, knowing us, knowing our past, sets up the present and the future.

THE PRESENT: WHO AM I?

The cult television series *The Prisoner*, starring Patrick McGoohan, was made in the 1960s, yet it is still being shown on British television and bought by fans on video. The hero of *The Prisoner* has no name. He is simply Number Six in a strange, self-contained world run by Number Two under orders from Number One. In the title sequence, our hero is seen crying out in defiance: 'I am not a number, I am a free man'.

His oppressor replies, 'I am Number Two and you are Number Six'. Many of us are in danger of making ourselves prisoners of an identity that others give to us, instead of being truly ourselves. How do you answer the question, 'Who am I'?

Are you confident you know the answer? It's easy to fall into a trap here. When we ask ourselves the question, 'Who am I?', the first thing that leaps into our minds is probably our name and what we do. 'I am Emma Fletcher and I am a Doctor.' 'I am Peter Smith and I mend cars.' 'I am Richard and I'm a househusband.' 'I'm called Rosetta and I run that ten million turnover business across the road with my name in pink neon lights above it.'

Who am I? The purpose of asking the question is to make a very simple point. We are not a combination of our name and occupation. We are not a mix of the external labels we bear. We are ourselves. Confidence is linked to identity. When we have a sense of who we are, it gives us solid ground to stand upon. If we do not know who we are, how are we to know what to do with our lives? We are not external labels. 'Single white female teacher' is a label, it is not us. We are not our job or our social status or our address or even the name our parents have given us. These things reveal information about us but they do not tell us who we are.

What we are talking about here are the inner sources of identity that are special to you and to me as individuals. Maybe you are musical, and your life would not be complete without music, whether making music or listening to it. You would not be happy in a world without music.

If you are a Christian, then your faith will be high on your list, if not at the top. Faith, after all, is not a garment you wear, but is essentially Christ in you. A Christian is a 'Christ-in' person, in New Testament language a 'new creation', where God has taken up residence.

What else are you thinking? Maybe you are a great lover of nature or art – these will be important parts of your life. Or perhaps sport is where you find you can express yourself. The question can produce a whole range of questions and answers which may only scrape the surface of who you are. Do not be afraid to explore these. This is a kind of self-audit in which you can start to see the many sides to your character. Hopefully you are already beginning to sense that there is more to you than you thought. Try to be positive and don't be afraid to feel good about yourself.

CLOTHES AS SKIN

I'm a great fan of the late Marshall McLuhan. Though he had something of a cult following in the sixties, during the seventies he went out of favour. McLuhan was an academic whose thinking on the media gave the English language such phrases as 'the medium is the message' and the concept of television turning the world into a 'global village'. Books like his *Understanding Media* were provocative and so packed with ideas that it was like watching a firework display. McLuhan has something relevant to say on our theme. It is this: look at how you dress – that says something about how you see yourself. Obvious it may be, but never overlook the obvious. Clothing is in a sense an extension of the skin, and can be seen both as a heat-control mechanism and as a means of defining the self socially. So look at how you dress and what it says about you.

As a teenager growing up in the sixties, I had a reputation amongst my friends for outrageous socks and ties. I remember with a mix of pleasure and deep embarrassment that I spent my university days wearing such audacious clothes as purple brushed nylon shirts. I was once stopped by a policeman for wearing my bicycle lights on my belt, wrapped around a 1947 fireman's jacket bought from an Army Surplus store. I shudder at the memory with a smile on my face.

Today I dress more conservatively, but my taste for outrageous ties and socks has stayed with me through the years. It is partly to meet the expectation of my friends and because it is now very much an expression of who I am. One of those two schoolfriends I referred to earlier is a country clergyman. He wears cardigans, tiepins and has leather patches on the elbows of his tweed jackets just as he has always done. Never a follower of fashion, he is utterly true to himself. He wears clothes that are comfortable, sensible and in which he can be himself. He would not look right in jeans and a tee shirt.

There is no right or wrong way for Christians to dress. What you wear is, however, a statement about yourself, so bear in mind the signals you give in the way you dress. You cannot fool people. Clothes are not a disguise or a mask – they are a consistent reflection of how you see yourself. People with low esteem often dress accordingly, avoiding any clothing that will draw attention to themselves. The more confident person will reflect their personality accordingly. It may be in a fashion, colour or style – whichever, it should be 'you'. Remember that icon of the eighties, the 'yuppie'. Suddenly half the young accountants and brokers in the City started to wear scarlet braces. The film *Wall Street* echoed the spirit of the age with Gordon Gekko's paean of praise to greed. 'Greed is good,' he proclaimed, and what a hollow ring that carries today. Where are the red braces now?

Hopefully, by this stage, you are finding that the process of looking at your past and your present situation is helping you to put yourself in relief. It's like jumping on board a satellite and looking at the Earth from space.

When we stand back a bit we can focus better and put our lives into context. It's the bigger picture we want. The relief map of our lives will carry many features from our past that contribute to the present. The face of a fisherman, lined and gnarled from the blasts of wind across the bows of his trawler is always more interesting to look at than the perfectly handsome but bland face of a teenage pop idol. I'd rather gaze into the face of Mother Theresa than that of Madonna!

With a proper sense of who we are and how we came to this time and place, and having reflected on how God came into our lives, let us turn our minds to what lies ahead. As Jesus sensed that the moment of truth was coming and his mission was drawing to its inevitable conclusion, Luke tells us: 'Jesus resolutely set out for Jerusalem. And he sent messengers on ahead, who went into a Samaritan village to get things ready for him' (Luke 9: 51–2). Jesus had made up his mind. He was confident about his purpose and mission and was not going to be sidetracked from it. As a student of the prophets, Jesus would have known the words from the writings of the prophet Isaiah: 'Because the Sovereign LORD helps me, I will not be disgraced. Therefore have I set my face like flint, and I know I will not be put to shame' (Isa. 50: 7).

THE FUTURE: WHERE AM I HEADING?

Do you have a sense of direction in your life? What are your goals? What is your guiding vision? We cannot expect to know where we are going in our life without taking some decisions about our future. It's like setting off on a car journey not knowing our destination. It can be exciting, but if we have to make diversions it can also be very exasperating. Nothing is more irritating than finding that the brilliant short cut takes us into a cul-de-sac or ends up in a one-way street. As someone who has driven the wrong way down a one-way street, take my word for it. Each of us needs to find a direction that best satisfies our hopes and aspirations. If it causes great inner turmoil and conflict, we should think again. It may still be right.

Don't assume that your direction is wrong. The probability is that you are already on the right path, using your gifts and talents and having a sense of personal fulfilment. That doesn't rule out the value of looking ahead and setting some targets. We will shortly move on to a very effective goal-setting exercise, but as we get on board the Tardis and start to look ahead, what do you see ahead for yourself?

Let me say right away, to avoid any misunderstanding, that we are talking about hopes and aspirations, not gazing into a crystal ball, which is never a good idea. It may be that we feel a little lost or bewildered and that all that is needed is a tug on the tiller to draw us back on to a true path. It may be that God gently wants to redirect us – or maybe a kick up the backside is nearer the mark! For most of us, perhaps, an exercise like this will confirm us on the path we are already taking or it will at least make us rethink it and perhaps set some new goals. We never rule out the possibility, however, that change can be dramatic and sudden. God is a God of surprises.

Take my friend, Sharon. Hers is a story of overnight change. She was not particularly happy in her job working in the export department of a large international manufacturer of personal care products. It had been on her mind for many months. She had prayed about it and asked God specifically if there was an alternative. Then suddenly, one morning, it struck her like a custard pie in the face. She woke up and said to herself, 'I want to be a teacher'. She had a modern languages degree, but in order to teach she would need to do a year's post-graduate Certificate of Education. This would in turn mean raising the finance for a year of student life. Sharon cannot explain why she had this sudden inner conviction that she must change job, other than to say that it was God speaking to her. But change direction she did. Two years on, Sharon has qualified and landed an excellent job as head of a language department.

As we face the future, I must stress again that for very many of us the call of God is not necessarily into pastures new, but to carry on where we are. Our local church has an extraordinary turnover rate. At one stage about 25 per cent of the church members were arriving or leaving the church every year – chasing new jobs, moving homes and enjoying the mobility of our modern society. But that still left a majority for whom continuity was the way ahead.

SETTING GOALS

If you have no sense at all of the future, then here is a simple goal-setting exercise that will help. I came across it in 1984 at the Lee Abbey Holiday centre in Lynton, North Devon. Interestingly, Lee Abbey was itself set up to restore and rebuild the shattered confidence of Christians after the Second World War. Many had lost their faith as they had seen loved ones die and witnessed the terrible acts of war. The founders of Lee Abbey set it up to heal the wounds of those whose faith was in pieces. Today a community is based there to help the weary find rest and to train church members.

I made a series of programmes for the BBC World Service on five different religious communities and Lee Abbey in Devon, England was one of them. Later on I was invited back as a guest speaker and on a third visit, we spent a family holiday there. A number of the holiday guests were using the time together to reflect on what they were doing. My wife and I had been youth leaders in our local church for five years and we wanted to use the holiday to stand back and consider whether or not it was the right time to step down as leaders.

We wanted to be confident we were making the right decision about our future. We did not find it easy to stand apart from our situation and take a more detached view. To help us and others in the same situation, one of the Lee Abbey farm estate team, called George, brought us together. He asked us some simple questions about our priorities. We found it very helpful at the time and I have used and adapted it in other situations. I call it the 'Diagnosis Test'.

THE DIAGNOSIS TEST

For this exercise to be effective, it helps if you can enter into the spirit of it by letting your imagination loose and doing a mental role-play. The situation is this: you have been to visit your doctor for a routine health check after a few weeks of not feeling too well. He examines you and as the health check proceeds, you begin to sense that all is not good. In fact, he's looking very grim. He sends you off to hospital and the next day calls you in for an appointment. He offers you a cup of tea and you know he's about to break some bad news.

First comes the bad news. You are told by your doctor that you have only three months to live. The news slowly sinks in. Your mind is full of questions. Picture yourself in this situation as best you can. If you have pencil and paper to hand, you may want to write down what is coming into your mind. Now focus on two specific questions. First, what are your priorities in the three months you have left to live? Second, how will you spend your time and energy? Take time to think this through in your mind. It may take five minutes or more.

Second comes the not-so-bad news. A week later, your doctor calls you back for another discussion of your condition. It turns out that the first diagnosis was too pessimistic – further tests suggest the condition is not quite as serious as it seemed at first. Medical opinion now reckons that you have not three months but a whole year to live. Now ask yourself the same two questions. Given a year to live, what are your priorities? How would you spend the last year of your life? Stop a moment and think about it. Maybe write down your conclusions.

Confidence in the Future

Third, and finally, comes the best news of all. The doctor has made a terrible mistake, samples have got mixed at the laboratory, the diagnosis was utterly wrong. Further checks have revealed that you are perfectly healthy and should have the rest of a long life to live. Once again, ask yourself the same key questions: What are your priorities now? What do you want to achieve in the days and months and years that stretch ahead? You might want longer now to collect your thoughts and write down what priorities you have.

The Diagnosis Test is a very helpful exercise, if a rather disturbing one. I hope it has proved helpful rather than traumatic to you. What have you learned about your priorities and values? How do they help you in the decisions you face? As you think about your future, has the way ahead become clearer – can you see the horizon?

Those who conduct these exercises always suggest you keep your results to yourself and reflect upon them, or maybe share them with your partner. I've still got what I wrote down back in 1984 when I went through this exercise. What I wrote then has stood up well to the test of time. Faced with three months to live I found that I wanted first of all to put my affairs in order and spend as much time as I could with my wife and family. I hadn't lost my sense of humour though – included on the list of things to do is 'sow early veg'! As a keen gardener, having three months to live was clearly not going to divert me from my hobbies. I also vowed to take my wife on a wonderful holiday, to spend some time of spiritual reflection on the Hebridean island of Iona (home of another Christian community), to see an eagle in the wild and, interestingly, to write a book.

My one-year list is short, with some specific personal projects including restoring the garden to maximum beauty and watching the entire series of Test cricket matches. But the real substance comes in what I have written down as goals for life. This is much more detailed and relates to my immediate family and to personal projects. These include making time to 'expand the "private" me by developing creative work such as writing and photography', and 'getting my body into good shape'. My overall life goal was 'to be as complete as I can in faith, as father and husband'. That was my Diagnosis Test in 1984. Try it, and I think you'll find it helps to clarify your priorities and goals.

As Christians, let us not forget that in trying to set goals for the future we are also seeking the will of God for our lives. In that sense, an exercise like this can help us to determine our calling. When Paul wrote to the church of Corinth, he underlined the fact that he saw himself as someone who had been given a specific task by God. In his case he was 'called to be an apostle' (1 Cor. 1: 1). And those to whom he wrote had their own calling 'to be holy' (1 Cor. 1: 2), which means set apart for God. This was not just an individual calling for every Christian, but was also one shared with other Christians. Paul writes that God has called us 'into fellowship with his Son Jesus Christ our Lord' (1 Cor. 1: 9).

Returning now to the Tardis time travel exercise, we have been examining the first question about the future, 'Where am I heading?' This should be clearer if we have done the Diagnosis Test. The second question is the one that addresses the issue of what lies in the path.

TRAFFIC ON THE WAY

I've suggested an image here to illustrate the obstacles that may lie ahead, deriving from the idea of travelling on life's journey. It is an all too familiar motoring image – the traffic jam. If your life were a circuit of the M25, what traffic lies in the way? Anyone who has driven round London's outer orbital motorway knows only too well that it is either a racetrack – with cars doing over eighty miles per hour on the inside lane and Porsches testing their acceleration in the fast lane – or a crawl. There are few experiences more frustrating than sitting in your car on a hot summer's day, going nowhere, with the traffic jammed as far as the eye can see. And you can guarantee that as you tune into the cricket on your car radio, English wickets will be tumbling at the same time. Even the voice of Freddie Trueman reminiscing on the past glories of English cricket will not bring a smile to your face.

Here we want to focus on what obstacles lie across our route to the future, blocking the way ahead. This may not be easy. We may immediately see some obstacle that is also a moral responsibility. It could be, for example, that we've always wanted to travel, but we live with a much-loved family member who is dependent upon us and cannot be left alone. Or we may find other blockages on our way. It could be ourselves. Perhaps we have an unfulfilled desire to explore the Highlands of Scotland, but we have never learned to drive. Are there personal or human barriers in the way? Do we have responsibilities we cannot shift? Is there an individual standing in our way? Or perhaps it is some personal difficulty that is holding us back? For example, a career move is blocked because your line manager is 'doing time' and waiting to retire. It may be a qualification we need. Perhaps we've always wanted to take up painting, but have not got round to having lessons to learn the technique.

When we ask ourselves these questions, let's make sure we include the spiritual dimension of our life too. It is when we are truly open to God's possibilities that he can break through and transform our parochialism into his grand vision for our life. Are there things holding us back in our prayer life? Does our spiritual life face obstacles or barriers to our growth and development?

REMOVING OBSTACLES

This is a hazardous zone in the journey. Sometimes the traffic jam ahead may be something we can do little about. Perhaps we have a major creative project ahead or a career move that will place a heavy commitment on our time. Suppose the obstacle is a responsibility we cannot escape. If it is something like looking after an aging parent or relative, the responsibility is a right and proper one, where a positive approach on our part can help us see it as a privilege and not a problem. The Americans like to say that every problem is an opportunity. The same person who may take up a lot of our time can sometimes be a means of releasing lots of time.

When my wife Gill gave birth to twins, with two children under seven already, the days were long and we were both in a state of perpetual tiredness. I was then working shifts as a Foreign Duty Editor in the BBC Radio Newsroom on a three-on three-off twelve-hour pattern. So I was either at home available to help or sitting in the Newsroom taking in the foreign correspondents' despatches. Though physically exhausting for Gill, it also turned out to be a time for spiritual restoration. She was forced to spend far more time at home so she expanded her horizons by using the gaps between feeding babies and changing nappies to collapse in a heap and read, reflect and recharge.

Five years of this has, in fact, given her a new sense of the need to explore her creative talents. To everyone's surprise Gill decided to do an 'A' level in Art. She also got sucked into the local school as a Parent Governor. What had seemed a 'blockage' – having twins and being tied to home – was in the end a liberating experience. She developed skills in that time which have led her in a new direction into the world of education. She has since completed her training to become a teacher.

Maybe there is a task which could in some way free up time for you elsewhere? Use your spiritual resources – of prayer and of regenerated thinking – to find a way around the obstacle. Then what seems to be an immovable object in the way can be a stepping stone on the journey.

To clear away the obstacles you have to be single-minded. A good illustration of this is the way in which the British sprinter Linford Christie won the 100 metres final at the Barcelona Olympics. As he crouched a split second before the start of the race, his eyes stood out like searchlights on a dark sea. When he came out of his blocks, his body radiating strength and the pursuit of a single goal, his eyes never wavered. He looked straight ahead and you knew that his mind was set on the single objective of winning Olympic Gold. Christie's powers of concentration are such that according to one sports writer, he actually believes he has bricks piled up on either side of his lane. He has such a narrow focus of attention that he sees nothing and nobody but the finishing line. And he's also able to time his performance so he is at his best on the big occasion. When the stakes are at their highest, Linford Christie is at his best. That's also why he's such an awe-inspiring figure as team captain.

How well we are able to cope with the obstacles in our journey through life will also give us an indication of our skills and our motivation. Whether these traffic jams are conscious and visible or subconscious and hidden around the corner, if they are slowing down our progress and holding us back, then let's make a big effort to do what we can to clear them out of our way. No obstacle is so great that we cannot tackle it; no mountain is so high that we cannot climb it. We can negotiate our way around a problem or we can confront it head-on. What is not a good idea is to avoid it. Only when the traffic jam is behind us and no longer in our way can we see our way ahead clearly.

PLANNING THE ROUTE

Gill is a brilliant navigator. She puts it down to her training as a Geographer at school and university. If she is driving the car and I am forced to navigate, it takes me the utmost concentration to follow the map closely. To Gill it is second nature. Give her a destination and a map and she'll come up with three ways of getting there, according to priorities. If time is important we go the quickest way. If it's a beautiful day and it doesn't matter how long it takes, we'll take the slower but more picturesque route. If the road is blocked with traffic, I can rely on her to find an alternative route.

We are not going to make it to our destination by accident. It helps to have a good idea of where we are heading and of the route we are going to take. When the former Republic of Yugoslavia wanted to overcome the international trade boycott, how did Serbia keep supplies coming in? By using the designated international waterway of the Rhine. Only Romania could stop goods getting through. To every problem there is a solution. Economic sanctions seldom work, because where there is a will, there is a way.

The blockage to our goal may lie within ourselves. Perhaps there is a painful memory holding us back – a change of job that did not work out, a personal relationship breakdown that has sapped our confidence in our own judgment. We may feel that we lack the drive and motivation to overcome a feeling of inertia or of being stuck where we are. Perhaps it's a deep-seated fear of stepping out into new terrain – a lack of security or self-confidence. Maybe we're not sure if we want to live with the consequences of change, or we feel that the risk is too great. Having established a sense of where we are heading and having identified the obstacles across our path, the next stage is to summon up the resources and aids we need to complete the journey. Here we can focus more on the spiritual resources as well as the material ones.

EQUIPMENT FOR THE JOURNEY

This is about the tools needed to do the job, the support systems we need, the human and spiritual resources we need to call upon. It may be a strategy of some sort. It could be a prayer strategy or a reallocation of time or a reordering of personal priorities; perhaps, finding time for creativity.

By this stage in the process I hope that you are well on the way to a useful degree of self-assessment. Remember that we can always use our nearest and dearest and our close friends to get feedback. It can be very illuminating, though not easy, to ask friends or family to put down in writing or to tell us to our face what they consider to be our personal strengths and what areas we need to work upon. Feedback, so long as it is positive and not an excuse for character assassination, can be a most useful tool.

Our personal resources include those who can help us, be they family or friends, church groups, or networks of old friends. 'Support systems' is the rather ugly phrase that those who know about these things like to use. It sounds like one of those Victorian corsets full of whalebone to hold our stomachs or waists in. We all need others to help us along the way. We all need moral support, encouragement or maybe financial support to embark on a new venture.

For me, one of the main resources I fall back upon is my network of Christian friends. There are two groups who meet regularly – both are places where I am surrounded by friends who care about me and will support me, as I try to support them. The first is the local church house group which meets fortnightly. The other is a long-standing group of old school and college friends who still live within reach of one another. This group meets over dinner in each other's homes once every six or seven weeks. We've been meeting on this basis for over fifteen years now, so we know each other and each other's churches pretty well. As my extended Christian family, it is these two groups on whom I know I can really count when the chips are down. That does not rule out good friends outside these groups, not least among colleagues at work. But if we are talking about spiritual resources, then those closest to hand will usually be of most value.

It may be that we need help from material sources as well. No one can launch a new business without some venture capital. Banks have to be cajoled, persuaded and bullied to give some financial backing. Partners may be needed to put in some capital to buy the necessary equipment to do the job. Whatever project you hope to take on, you will need the right resources to do the job, whether it is personal skills, human or financial resources.

As important as any of these are spiritual resources. This is linked to a good and healthy relationship with God. The joints of the spiritual engine need to be greased with prayer, lubricated with worship and renewed with Bible reading. Without the discipline of prayer, our relationship with God becomes distant instead of close. Without worship and meeting together with other Christians, the tank soon runs dry. Without a regular input of Bible reading the Christian has to fall back on memory and a valuable daily source of sustenance is taken away.

You need support for your internal life to complete this journey. You need the support of friends who understand you and can give you moral support. You also need the assurance that God is working in your life to help you achieve your goals and, therefore, ultimately his purposes too. How many of us have found personal and inner strength from the knowledge that 'in all things God works for the good of those who love him, who have been called according to his purpose' (Rom. 8: 28). Paul does not write this as a hypothesis or as a strategy but as an undisputed fact of life. 'We know,' he says – it is true.

LIFE'S STAIRCASE

What have you discovered about yourself? What have you learned about your personal voyage in life? On your physical and spiritual journey, what landmarks have you noted? What lies on the horizon? Are you happy with your situation? Do you want to change direction at all or chart a new course? Are the sheets covered with jottings, or are they staring back at you blank and bare? Was it hard to find things to say, or did you find your mind beginning to spin as the thoughts tumbled out?

What we have done in this chapter is to embark on a journey into ourselves, in preparation for being more effective as Christians in the world in which we live. Think of standing on a staircase. The first step is our past, the second step our present. We are about to step on to the third step – the future. We are not alone. As a Christian we have God as our fellow traveller, we have his Holy Spirit living within us to guide us and direct us and empower us. He makes our lives fruitful and gives us gifts to use and talents to invest in the future. We are not talking about a solo voyage here, but about a partnership and that makes it all the more exciting.

Behind us, helping us climb the staircase, we will hopefully have the supportive hands of family and friends, encouraging us onwards and upwards. We have assessed the kind of person we are, and have got to know our internal community a little better. We've thought about the direction we want to take on this journey and we've seen some potential obstacles ahead. We've decided to harness the resources available to

Confidence in the Future

us to overcome the difficulties. Let us now go forward with renewed purpose, ready to live our life and our faith with confidence. In the words of the infamous opening of *Star Trek*, 'To boldly go . . .'

6
THE CONFIDENCE EATERS

There was much rivalry in ancient Greece between the cities of Sparta and Athens. Sparta was the capital city of a territory called Laconia. On one occasion the Athenians sent their enemies in Sparta a threatening message: 'Unless you do as we wish we shall make war on you and, if we defeat you, shall lay waste your country, raze your cities to the ground, slaughter all your men of military age and enslave your women and children'. The Spartans were pretty useful themselves in the art of warfare. To their enemies in Athens was sent a defiant, single word in reply: 'If . . .' Not for nothing did these people give the English language two words which this reply illustrates – spartan and laconic.

It is hard to carry conviction if we are riddled with doubt. To secure the high ground and express our views and share our faith with confidence, it helps if we can be sure in our own minds that what we stand for is true. I'm not talking about blind dogmatism which ignores what others say – that is of no use to anybody. What I'm talking about is confidence that Christianity is based on solid foundations of history and not on myth or invention. In the next chapter we will re-examine the basis of our faith and its origins. In this chapter I want go back one stage further and look at the influences that have undermined Christian confidence in recent years.

Some people end up thinking that faith is flawed, that the foundations of the Christian faith somehow might rest on dodgy foundations which are crumbling away. If you look closely at those foundations, you will in fact find that, far from being cracked or fatally flawed, they stand up well to any amount of stress from outside. No Christian has any reason to abandon the historical basis of our faith or belief in the supernatural. There are answers to the questions being raised and there is ample evidence to support what Christians believe. In the next two chapters, we will look at the reasons underlying the loss of confidence in the Christian faith and then see why there is, on historical and archaeological grounds, every reason for the Christian to remain confident. Seldom before has such a mass of data been available to confirm what Christians have believed through the centuries. But at the end of the day, faced with the evidence, every person must make up their own mind.

Only in recent years, I would argue, have Christians begun to respond to the challenge of living in a society which is no longer really Christian in anything but name. Modern Britain is a predominantly secular, multi-faith and, some would argue, post-Christian society. It has a sense of its Christian heritage and past, but is less certain than it once was of its Christian values. What can be done to redress that loss of confidence? How can we move forward off the defensive and back on to the attack? How can we be sure that what we believe is true and can withstand the challenges from wherever they come?

CLAIMING THE HIGH GROUND

The Christian Church can no longer afford the luxury of sitting back and not getting involved in our society. Christians cannot hope to have an influence in our world if we shut ourselves off into a ghetto mentality. We need to make our presence felt and get our ideas across. We need to show the truth of what we believe by having a positive cutting edge in society. We need to be identifying the issues that count and playing our part in our churches and communities. It is time to reclaim the high ground, to lead by example and to reflect the love of Christ to others through our own lives.

We can swim with the sharks in our society and not be eaten up before breakfast! It's time for Christians to stop being over-defensive or retreating into our shells. We must let those around us know where we stand, not by thrusting our beliefs down their throats but by quietly and effectively living our faith. In the words of Peter the disciple, 'In your hearts set apart Christ as Lord. Always be prepared to give an answer to everyone who asks you to give the reason for the hope that you have. But do this with gentleness and respect, keeping a clear conscience' (1 Pet. 3: 15–16).

When I was a university student I went through this process myself. I wanted to be sure in my own mind that the Christian faith I professed could stand up to the most rigorous intellectual questioning. I'm not suggesting that the existence of God is something that can be proved in a forensic sense, but it is equally absurd to think that faith is a 'blind leap into the dark', in which all intellectual honesty has to be sacrificed for belief to be possible. The origins of Christianity will quite happily stand up to historical scrutiny. Our faith is not based on lies or supposition, but on a historical figure of flesh and blood whom millions of Christian believers worship as God.

More than that, the Christian faith affirms that Jesus Christ is not dead and buried, but was killed on a cross by means of crucifixion, his body placed in a burial cave under Roman guard, only later to be seen alive in various locations by hundreds of witnesses. In other words, Jesus rose from the dead and is alive today. This might sound extraordinary, but when you look at the evidence of history it is the explanation that makes most sense. Christians today claim to have a living relationship with that same Jesus. Jesus is alive in Christian believers and alive through his Spirit in the churches. No one has to sell their intellect to become a Christian. Faith in Jesus Christ is not a second-rate creed bought at a discount off the back of a lorry. Any truth worth having must stand up for itself.

I wanted to find out for myself whether or not the Gospels could be treated seriously as a historical source for the life of Jesus. As part of my degree I had to learn first-century Greek, so I was able to examine the documents as they were written and get back to the basics. I came through the process, which occupied the last two years of my degree, confident that the

Gospels are reliable and trustworthy. Some of the questions that Christians need to answer – such as the reliability of the Gospels as evidence and the lateness of their writing – I will deal with shortly.

Where there is honesty there will always be room for doubt. Any Christian who has never questioned his or her faith or had doubts, I would suspect of not being totally honest with him or herself. It is quite another thing to be so racked with doubt, that we are left in a position of indecision or even indifference to our faith. We need not be afraid to address our doubts and to examine zones of doubt and difficulty with honesty and integrity. We will always have doubts and questions on some things. There will always be areas of life which defy rational explanation, especially on questions of suffering and death. But none of this need take away our underlying Christian confidence. Not for nothing has Christianity survived two thousand years. The fact is that for millions of Christians today as yesterday, the Christian message is relevant, topical, powerful, life-changing and true.

THE PIRANHAS OF FAITH

Let me identify three of the biggest confidence eaters confronting Christians today. I would describe these as:

(a) Secularism – the gradual removal of God from our everyday lives, the sense that the fate of humanity lies in our own hands alone. This sees religion as irrelevant and often damaging.
(b) Science – the sense that science either disproves faith or makes faith irrelevant. The Archbishop of Canterbury, George Carey, told a conference in Swanwick that there was an unspoken modern assumption that religious faith and a scientific outlook were implacably opposed. 'One deals in values and the other in fact,' he said, 'but we have given way too readily. There was no need to give so much ground.'

(c) Suffering and disaster – the age-old problem of how Christians can believe in a God of love in a world of death and suffering.

WHERE GOD SEEMS IRRELEVANT

There are many different ways of living in our world today and of interpreting what goes on in it. A secular view of life is one which is sceptical of religious truth. One of the telltale signs of creeping secularism is in our schools. Now I am not a great advocate of religious education where it is badly taught, carried out by teachers of no faith who are doing it out of duty. But I do believe that every child should at least be given a proper understanding of what Christians believe and why, so that they can make up their own minds on a decent basis, rather than on hearsay. Recent research in schools suggests that religious education is in a sorry state.

The *Times Educational Supplement*, December 25th, 1992, reports that, despite legislation that there should be a collective and daily act of worship in schools which is 'mainly Christian', 'Britain's Christian traditions are being ignored in schools with religious assemblies and hymn singing under threat'. The *TES* survey of over one hundred schools, primary and secondary, suggests that many are flouting the government's directive. One school in five said they would refuse to meet the wishes of education ministers that RE classes should reflect Britain's Christian traditions. A spokesperson for the National Curriculum Council said, 'RE is being marginalised and there is a great deal of concern about its integrity as a subject'. Only four in every ten primary schools surveyed and just 15 per cent of secondary schools held collective acts of worship at least four times a week. The law requires this for all pupils every day. Prayers have been dropped in 35 per cent of the secondary schools and almost two-thirds have stopped singing hymns. The picture is more encouraging to supporters of the Christian tradition in primary schools, with prayers said in 88 per cent of schools and hymns sung in 74 per cent.

SECULAR VIEWS

Within the secular framework there are as many views of humanity as there are craters on the moon. All of these help to undermine Christian confidence. There is what I shall call the 'secular optimist' view of man. This sees people as the highest product of the evolutionary process, a species with unlimited potential and intelligence. We have the brains to unravel the genetic secrets of life and to place one of our own species on the surface of the moon. Yet somehow human beings just cannot get it right – our primitive urges get the better of us. This view sees people as a species that has evolved with a moral responsibility, yet is still a long way from controlling its nature. I call this the secular optimist view, because it argues that human beings are getting better all the time.

To the secular optimist, evolution is not a theory but a fundamental key to understanding human nature. This view is agnostic about God: God may be the source of our conscience, but may just as easily be a human invention, a God of the gaps to fill the spaces in our knowledge. This view is optimistic, because it believes that, at the end of the day, despite all the evidence to the contrary, reason and human intelligence will triumph. The instinct to survive will open our eyes to our own folly. Faced with extinction, humanity will draw back from the abyss and embrace universal brotherhood. Technology holds the key.

The 'secular pessimist' view of people is in many ways a more honest one. This sees human beings as a cosmic accident, not created by a personal, infinite God, but as a result of some primeval accident at the dawn of time. This view reduces us to a mere combination of chemicals, so that the deepest human feelings, such as love, are no more than a chemical or biological reaction. We are the sum total of our genes and our environment. The human body is no more than a carbon-based unit. Secular pessimism finds its spiritual home in the French school of thought, known as existentialism. In this view, God is dead so humans are free. Life has no purpose or meaning, so the sooner we face up to that the better. We live for the moment alone. Religious faith is a futile exercise, an attempt to escape from the reality that death is the end. It is rather like the old joke that there are only three certainties in life: life itself, death and taxes. The secular pessimist view has no place for God and offers no hope or purpose. It is a position that ultimately leads to despair. Death is the end of our existence, there is no ultimate meaning to anything, our actions are of no lasting significance. The difficulty of the secular pessimist position is that life without hope and meaning is intolerable.

NEW AGE THINKING

A third, and more recent, view of seeing the world is what might loosely be called the 'new age' view. 'New age' itself is an umbrella term that covers a whole range of activities and beliefs. Some aspects – homeopathy, for example – are not particularly new or controversial. For generations people in Britain at least, including prominent members of the Royal Family, have used medicines derived from herbs and plants. Other aspects are of a different order altogether, some of it not so much 'new age' as 'old age', returning to a pre-Christian fascination with 'mother earth' and attributing great powers to inanimate objects such as rocks and crystals. We might find people turning to the stars for astrological guidance. Some drift into occult areas, turning to tarot cards. Unlike the other secular views, new agers do acknowledge the spiritual dimension to life. Many believe death is not the end but part of a cycle of events, in which reincarnation is a distinct possibility. There are techniques for self-discovery such as 'channelling' into your inner psyche.

New agers see people as an indelible part of the natural order of things. New age thinking gives a sacred quality to the natural order of things – referring to 'mother Nature' and seeing human beings as a part of the natural order, but not giving God the credit or the responsibility. Through the new age window on life, everything we do gains significance because of its impact on the environment and on our planet. We are part of Spaceship Earth, hurtling through the cosmic universe, trying to touch the forces that control our lives.

For new agers, if there is a God, he is not one who has revealed himself fully in the life of Christ. Rather, he is a god-within-you. The popularity of this approach is in itself an indictment of Christians for failing to present Christ and the claims of Christ simply and clearly. New age ideas are filling a spiritual need to which the Christian faith has real answers instead of the spurious cul-de-sacs and diversions which thrive under the new age umbrella.

It is easy to see why new age thinking can appeal to those who are seeking for spiritual reality but reject the faith of the past. It is almost an attempt to return to a pagan and pre-Christian world. No wonder some claim that the Christian era is over – the Age of Pisces the Fish – and that the Age of Aquarius is dawning.

All three of these secular views have an influence and a following in our society today. All of them have contributed to the undermining of the confidence of the churches and of Christians in what they believe. These three views can rub off on Christians too. We share the secular optimist view of the human predicament on our planet. We share the sense of responsibility for our stewardship of God's created order, but we cannot agree that humanity is getting better. The history of this century suggests otherwise. More blood has been shed and more wars waged on a global scale in the twentieth century than in any other. The secular pessimist view is one that we who are Christians utterly reject. It leaves humanity with no hope, no meaning, no basis for morality and it offers only despair and angst. It stands for everything the Christian gospel opposes. Instead of faith we have fear, instead of hope we have despair, instead of life having purpose, it is absurd. It does not feed our creative and spiritual side; it suffocates and destroys.

The new age view of life is one that Christians can in part find attractive at a superficial level. Here human beings are more than animals: we have spirits too, but we are still left to our own devices. We are open to outside forces and influenced by them, but in this view, God is rarely defined and certainly not the personal, infinite God of Christianity. No blend of eastern mysticism and alternative therapies can substitute for the utterly realistic view offered by the Christian faith.

THE CHRISTIAN VIEW

How do we counter these views which hint towards God or rely on human beings as the supreme species, but which offer no hope, certainty or purpose in life? It is time for Christians to reclaim the ground on which our faith stands. We need to restate our total confidence in the Christian view of humanity. It is realistic, it is positive and it holds in its heart not just the seeds of faith but the hope of the human race fulfilling its God-given potential. We hold that each person is made in God's image and is set apart from the animal kingdom. This is not to support or to deny the theory of evolution. It is possible to reconcile a Creator God with a universe that is changing and developing and in which God is involved at every stage. But evolution, like all theories, has its merits and its flaws, its supporters and its attackers. Opponents of evolution see it as a denial of God the Creator and a theory with more holes than a Swiss cheese. They point to species like the mudfish that show no evidence of development over time and to the absence of a 'missing link' between human and animal species. Others hold that God started a process and sustains it. His 'sustaining' role is to use his creative power at every stage in the natural order, including change and developments within species. Wherever cells divide or change and animals gain new characteristics, we see the hand of the Creator at work in the evolutionary process. Here creation and evolution go hand in hand: they do not rule each other out.

The idea that God created the entire world with every species exactly as it exists today and totally untouched by time is surely as hard to believe as the idea that everything has evolved by random chance alone. The universe shows every sign of a creative mind and a sense of purpose behind it. I have heard it described by the Christian theoretical physicist,

Professor John Polkinghorne, as 'rationally beautiful and shot through in its fabric and structure with signs of a mind'.

It is absurd to think that creation stopped on Day One of the universe. That is to see God as a cosmic watchmaker who, once the world is made, sits back and lets it tick away for eternity. God is involved in the affairs of humanity and the world he has made. The Bible is a record of God's interventions in all our lives, to the extent of taking on human flesh and becoming human himself in Jesus Christ. Jesus is the best evidence of all that God is intimately locked into the nature of humanity and that the Christian view of humanity is essentially good – marred, yes, but soundly made in the image of a loving Creator God.

Evolution's role, if we give it one, is to be a God-driven vehicle for the natural order of events, with God involved at each stage of mutation and development. It has to be said, too, that if we look at ourselves, we see human beings living longer, growing taller and using God-given medical skills to survive and beat illnesses and conditions that would have killed our grandparents.

'Made in God's image' means more than looking good. It means that we carry within our make-up the hallmarks and characteristics of God himself. A piece of silver or gold produced in Britain is instantly identifiable by the hallmarks stamped on it to provide proof positive of its quality and origin. So, too, our natures reflect that of God, yet we know how that image has become tarnished.

What has gone wrong? The bald fact is that we fail to come up to standard. We fail to meet our own standards of thought and behaviour, let alone those of God. We are all like Robin Hood on an off day when we aim high but we fall short. The Bible uses the word 'sin' to describe this basic human condition. It means our relationship with God is marred. The exception is Jesus himself, whom we find described as 'the radiance of God's glory and the exact representation of his being' (Heb. 1: 3). Jesus is the key that unlocks the door back to God. To be restored to what God wants us to be, to reflect more of his image if you like, is what the gospel is all about. For us it is a process of personal renewal. All sorts of God-words are used to describe this – from 'salvation' and 'redemption' to 'atonement'. At the heart of all three words is the idea that God wants us back in a full and proper relationship with himself and that all that was necessary to make this possible has been done by Jesus. It is as if God has sent out his own rescue mission to bring us back into his orbit with Jesus as the rescue vehicle.

It was Jesus's death and his resurrection that prepared the ground. Jesus himself died the death we all deserve for the lives we lead and took our weaknesses and failures upon himself. So it is that Paul pleads with his readers in the sea port of Corinth, 'We implore you on Christ's behalf: Be reconciled to God. God made him who had no sin to be sin for us' (2 Cor. 5: 20–21). Our response is one of repentance and faith, turning away from our old life and turning to Christ in faith. So we find in the Christian view of humankind that we are made in the image of God, reflecting his character. We see how we ought to be in the self-giving life of Jesus of Nazareth. We see what we are truly like in relation to him.

We also have a special and separate place in the order of things with the animals and other living things with whom we share our planet. We are in relationship to them because of the nature of the created order: we are inextricably bound up together. But our nature is quite different from that of the animals. In common with our Maker we have minds that can reason, a moral awareness and conscience. We use language and have a sense of beauty, a sense of responsibility to the world in which we live and to one another. All of this supports the Bible's view that human beings are more than just equal partners with animals and plants, we have a unique place within creation.

There is a deeper consequence to human beings falling out with God. The result is a breakdown in our relationships at every level. It means that mankind's relationship with God has gone wrong and needs to be rectified in Christ. It means that we fall out with one another. It also spells out disaster for our environment, as we lose touch with our proper relationship with our world. We exploit it and its resources to the point where our own planet is threatened by the ways in which we mistreat it. We live in a world in which people starve in Africa while the European Community destroys surplus food crops because we grow too much. We have not yet devised the means to feed the poor and to save the starving. We cut down rain forests and destroy animal species and plants that may carry life-saving drugs for diseases that destroy us. None of us needs to be reminded that animal species like the blue whale, the panda, the tiger and the elephant may not still be around when our great-grandchildren walk the Earth.

So we see the inevitable consequences of our disjointed relationships. All of us suffer the effects of the Fall. Our bodies fail, our minds fade and our spirits are corrupted. But we are capable of renewal by grace through faith in Jesus Christ (Eph. 2: 8). He has done all that is necessary to reconcile us to God in his death and resurrection. That is the heart of the Christian gospel. As Christians, we are renewed. For us, death is not the end of life. Our minds and spirits become refreshed and renewed by God. Our nature comes under new management. We still fail and make a hash of things, but guilt and failure are replaced by forgiveness and renewal. We find our capacity to love enlarged by God and our spiritual lives take off as we discover the power of prayer and get to know who God is.

What, then, is a human being? A naked ape and no more? A cosmic traveller in search of himself? A biological accident with no ultimate purpose? An absurdity without meaning? No, we are made to worship God and to enjoy him. In the words of the Psalmist: 'What is man that you are mindful of him, the son of man that you care for him? You made him a little lower than the heavenly beings and crowned him with glory and honour. You made him ruler over the works of your hands; you put everything under his feet' (Ps. 8: 4–6).

SCIENCE AND FAITH

One of my colleagues was surprised to discover that I am a Christian believer. 'No one believes any of that any more,' he said. 'Science has proved it's all nonsense.' Science has

The Confidence Eaters

become for many people the great destroyer of religious faith. In a secular world view, science deals with the physical and material which can be demonstrated, and religious faith is based on unproven leaps of fantasy that have nothing to do with the real world. In a 'scientific' view, everything can be explained and there is no place for religion, an invention to fill the gaps in our knowledge. Worse than that, faith is a fraud, and a damaging one at that, which in its delusion has caused countless wars and much suffering. That is a caricature of how many people see the Christian faith from what they see as a scientific point of view.

In fact, such thinking is a travesty of both science and faith and is based on a fundamental misunderstanding. A line must be drawn between science, which deals with present reality, and faith, which deals with questions of ultimate reality. Science tries to answer the question 'How?' It cannot answer the deeper question 'Why?'

I asked a Physics teacher from one of the country's top schools for his opinion on why many Christians' confidence has been undermined by science. 'The modern scientist,' he told me, 'has to grapple with a discipline based on a colossal body of knowledge expressed in a code which is verbally, and often mathematically, extremely complex. Small wonder that most of us look in at science from the outside and see something which is inaccessible and intimidating. As Christians, we can easily be deceived into conceding claims which science does not, or should not, make.'

This mistake can lead to a bigger one. We can be so impressed with the progress of science and overawed by the latest discoveries, be it chaos theory or trying to unravel the mysteries of the origin of the universe, that science itself becomes a substitute for God. In the words of my friend the Physics teacher, 'We can be fooled into thinking that science marginalises God, substituting rational explanations for theological ones and rendering the God revealed pre-scientifically by the Bible obsolete in the modern world of telecom and infotech'.

'Big Bang shapes up to God's Grand Design' ran the headline in the *Guardian* on February 15th, 1993, for its report on the American Association for the Advancement of Science 1993 meeting in Boston. At the meeting Professor Ian Barbour told delegates that recent scientific findings placed God firmly back on the scientific agenda:

> Among the many possible universes consistent with Einstein's equations ours is one of the few in which the arbitrary parameters are right for the existence of anything resembling organic life . . . We can still stand in awe of a universe in which galaxies and life and consciousness and self-conscientiousness came into being. Evidence from cosmology does not provide a proof for the existence of God but it is consistent with belief in a cosmic design that is not pre-determined in all its details.

Interestingly, Professor Barbour is a former Professor of Physics who now holds the Chair of Religion at Carleton College, Northfield, Minnesota.

Professor Joel Primack, a cosmologist at the University of California, detected what he sees as a mystic dimension to recent discoveries about the origin of the universe. One was the 'inflation' theory, in which space expanded faster than light for a billionth of a second after the 'Big Bang' and then settled into the expanding universe seen today. Another sees the universe as a tiny bubble in a violent cascade of eternal energy. All of this carries echoes of the Christian view of God as eternal, omnipresent and endlessly creative. In Professor Primack's words, 'this is science but it is the kind of stuff religious mystics dreamed about' (The *Guardian*, February 15th, 1993).

Is God now redundant, killed off by science? Don't you believe it! Christian doctrine is not trying to explain who lit the blue touchpaper of the 'Big Bang', through which the universe supposedly began, but deals with why things exist. God is as much the Creator today as he was then. The laws of Physics are not disjointed and random, but are ordered. The hope of man rests not in the outcome of the universe, but it rests beyond death and decay in God himself. Death and transience are built into the fabric of the universe.

The Confidence Eaters

It is a mistake to think that the Christian faith is being undermined by science because science seems to be infringing on territory which we have assumed to belong to God. I remember hearing in a church back in 1969 the opinion that God would never let a human land on the moon as that would be some kind of blasphemy. Humanity was trespassing on forbidden territory. In fact, as we know, many astronauts have found the experience to be of tremendous spiritual power. One of them, the late James Irwin, found that his voyage to the moon in the *Apollo 15* became his own spiritual pilgrimage. In his book *To Rule the Night* he describes how, after the flight, he was baptised at a Baptist church in Houston and his life was changed.

> I tell people that God has a plan for them. I say that if God controls the universe with such infinite precision, controlling all the motion of the planets and the stars, this is the working out of a perfect plan for outer space. I believe that He has the perfect plan for the inner space of man, the spirit of man.*

Science has a legitimate task to seek out answers and explanations. None of this need threaten Christian belief. God is not a God of the gaps, providing a convenient explanation for the things we don't understand. If that were all, then it would follow that as the gaps in our understanding of things shrink, then so would God. As science explores the 'how' questions and finds answers, Christians should marvel that more of God's astonishing design is being uncovered. The 'why' questions will remain and only the Christian world view can offer satisfactory answers.

My friend the Physics teacher puts it like this.

> As for God being out of date in our age of machines, is it not abundantly clear that we need him just as much as ever? Technological advances enable mankind to do

---

* James B. Irwin with William A. Emerson Jr, *To Rule the Night*, Hodder & Stoughton, 1973, p. 23.

things undreamed of in past times. Look at your car, however sleek or battered it may be, and imagine the history-changing effect you could have had by driving it on to the battlefield in 1066. But think too of the invisible gases emanating from the exhaust pipe and thus making your small contribution to global warming, a problem created by science and awaiting a scientific solution. Human problems exist a-plenty. How absurd it would be to suggest that God does not understand them or care about them. It is perfectly reasonable to look to God and at the same time but in a different way to look to science, for solutions.

There is something of a gulf to be bridged to bring science and faith closer together. Professor John Polkinghorne has gone a long way towards this in his various books. He is one of Cambridge University's top academics who, relatively late in life, became a priest in the Church of England. He has stayed in Cambridge and the academic world and is now President of Queen's College, Cambridge. Professor Douglas Spanner, a Botanist at Bedford College, has pursued a similar path and also became a clergyman after a distinguished career in science.

The novelist Susan Howatch hopes to speed up the process of demonstrating how science and faith are compatible by providing Cambridge University with funding (from her sales of over twenty million books) to set up the Starbridge Lectureship in Theology and Natural Science. Interviewed on Radio 4's *Sunday* programme, she said, 'I hope it'll produce much wisdom and much information on the subject of science and religion, the interplay between the two. A lot of people are trapped in the mindset of forty/fifty years ago and think that science killed religion off, but this is absolutely untrue'. When the lectureship was announced, she said that she wants to 'strike a blow for theology to show that religion is not dead but complements scientific discovery'. Theology has changed her life. Her first fortune was made writing novels such as *Penmarric*. But all the trappings of wealth and the hedonistic lifestyle which followed left her feeling unsatisfied. 'Theology revolutionised my life. It's integrated my personality, it's stretched my intellect and it's created a happiness that endures.' The University's Vice Chancellor, Professor Sir David Williams, expressed his delight at her 'most generous and imaginative proposal which offers the opportunity to advance in an area of significance to both science and theology'. Susan Howatch hopes that the establishment of the lectureship will result in 'science and theology no longer seen as opposed but as complementary – two aspects of one truth'.

Although science can be a confidence eater for some Christians, it need not be. It will only do so if we let it. If we make a clear distinction in our minds between the different questions to which science and faith seek answers, we will not go wrong. Science has its limits. Science cannot, as Professor Stephen Hawking mischievously suggests in his book on time, know the mind of God.

OUR LOSS OF WONDER

Scepticism about the scientific value of faith is fed by the insatiable appetite to find answers to questions to which there are no easy answers. There is little room in today's world for a sense of wonder, at least not in Western culture. When I was a child, I had a keen interest in astronomy, corresponding regularly with Patrick Moore and charting the movements of planets through the constellations. On our family holidays on the Sussex coast, I would stay up through the night with a telescope studying the night sky, while my father fished from the beach. It is a precious childhood memory. I couldn't do that today because of the street lighting. This might sound odd, but it is so significant for astronomers that *The Times* devoted a page of its 'Weekend' section on December 19th, 1992 to this single issue of light pollution with an article entitled 'Stealing the night away'.

Science writer Nigel Hawkes posed the question: 'When did you last see the night sky packed with stars from horizon to horizon?' He tells how, in satellite pictures from space, the lights used by fishermen in the Sea of Japan to draw squid to the surface can be seen as a brilliant pool of light. Israel appears as a brilliant white strip and Germany, like Japan, has huge splurges of light visible from space. 'We have,' Hawkes writes, 'allowed our view of the heavens to be taken from us without noticing, as we allowed the air to be polluted by smoke and the environment by pesticides. A whole dimension of human experience has been spirited away.'

It is not just the evidence of our own eyes which confirms this. How many of us searched in vain for Halley's Comet, supposedly an object visible to the naked eye, in the summer of 1986? Even with the aid of binoculars, I could barely make out a fuzzy blur. The astronomers have even fled from the countryside and have taken their telescopes with them. The finest instrument of the Royal Greenwich Observatory has over time been moved from Greenwich to Sussex and is today located in the Canary Islands. Light pollution is to blame – glare from badly designed street lights that throw light up into the sky instead of on to the ground where we need it. Alan MacRobert, associate editor of *Sky and Telescope* magazine is quoted in the article in *The Times*: 'The absolute majesty, the incredible power of a truly dark, star-packed sky was part of the experience of all of humanity throughout all of human history. Now in developed countries, it's practically unknown'.

SUFFERING AND DISASTER

How does personal faith stand up to personal loss and suffering? Sometimes faith can be shattered by a personal loss or a painful experience. There are no quick and easy answers to the cry from the heart of 'Why, Lord?' Do you remember what happened to the Australian family, the Chamberlains? They were on a camping holiday at Ayers Rock in the outback when their baby daughter, Azaria, disappeared. They claimed she had been taken by a wild dog, a dingo, but they ended up accused of murdering her. The mother, Lindi, was eventually found guilty of murdering her baby daughter and sentenced to life imprisonment with hard labour. Her husband, pastor of a Seventh Day Adventist Church, was given a suspended sentence for being an accessory to murder. It was eight years after the disappearance that their torment ended when a piece of Azaria's clothing was found near the site. This was proof that the baby had been taken by a dingo. Their names were cleared and Lindi Chamberlain freed from jail. Many times they asked the question: why did God allow this nightmare to happen to them? There is no answer.

'Queen Honours Men of Courage' ran the banner headline across the front page of the *Daily Mail* on Thursday, December 31st, 1992. After a year in which two entertainers stared death in the face, Leslie Crowther was made a CBE and Roy Castle an OBE in the New Year Honours list of 1993. The paper went on to describe Roy Castle as the 'multi-talented celebrity who won a new generation of fans through his *Record Breakers* programme became a national inspiration with his high-profile battle against lung cancer.'

It had clearly been a remarkable year for Roy Castle. In his words it had been 'a year of highs and lows and, in a funny way, one of the best years of my life. I seem to have won a lot of awards this year, but it's the illness that has brought everything to the top'.

Just a week before the award was announced, I found myself taking part in a special Celebration of Christmas alongside Roy Castle, organised by the Arts Centre Group at All Souls Church, Langham Place in London. For twenty-five years, the ACG has provided a forum for Christians who are professional in the arts – actors, artists, dancers, writers and broadcasters – to meet together and encourage one another. This occasion was typical of their work, creative, positive and confident. The highlight for me was hearing Roy and Fiona Castle talking about their traumatic year. Here was a man who was told he was terminally ill with lung cancer, defying the odds and talking about his experience. His months of treatment and of coming to terms with the prospect of death had been under the scrutiny of the national press.

During this time he had shown enormous courage and spoken openly of his Christian faith. During the treatment all his hair had fallen out and he suffered the most terrible and painful mouth ulcers. Roy Castle believed his lung cancer was caused by passive smoking during countless gigs playing his trumpet in smoky clubs. It would be perfectly understandable if Roy Castle had become bitter and disillusioned by the experience, but the reverse was true: 'It's the best thing that ever happened to me. When someone says you have three months to live, you see everything clearly'.

His first reaction to the news of the seriousness of his condition was one of total numbness. Then he began to see his experience through the light of his faith in Jesus Christ. It was as if God had been saying to him in the past: 'Sit on the bench – I'll call you out to play when it's your turn,' and this was it. He said that he had 'always wanted to do something for the Lord' and this was the opportunity. He had heard someone describe problems as 'growth activators', and for him this was a time of growing faith. His illness had given him a platform to share his faith with others. 'We've both grown a lot through this,' said Fiona Castle, as she talked of the faith they share and the confidence they have in God.

This is not 'blind faith', this is faith tested by the fire of imminent death through lung cancer. The initial treatment was effective and it seemed that the cancer had abated. Roy Castle knew it might return, and it did, but his faith, far from being shaken by the experience, grew through it.

It is hard to imagine being told that you have only three months to live and coming through that with confidence and with your faith not just intact, but strengthened. Confidence in the face of suffering requires courage and faith. Yet it is possible. Look at the Western hostages held for so long in Beirut.

The Archbishop of Canterbury's envoy, Terry Waite, suffered as much as anyone could endure at the hands of his captors. His Christian convictions and the way in which his faith helped him to survive under the most difficult duress has been well documented. Less well known is Terry Anderson's story. The American Associated Press journalist and bureau chief in Beirut was held for almost seven years, longer than any of the other hostages. In that time he was moved to nearly twenty different locations, from underground cells to secret hiding places in Beirut, Southern Lebanon and the notorious Bekaa Valley. Much of that time he was blindfolded. Like all the hostages, he suffered physical and verbal abuse, beatings and torture:

> The humiliation of such treatment and the thousands of major and minor humiliations that followed, were harder to deal with. Often I objected, loudly and vehemently. Sometimes it worked; more often it just brought more punishment. The only real defence was to remember that no one could take away my self-respect and dignity. I found consolation and counsel in the Bible I was given in the first few weeks. Not 'this is just a test' kind of consolation, but comfort from the real, immediate voices of people who had suffered greatly, and in ways that seemed to go so close to what I was going through. I read the Bible more than 50 times in those first few years. The other most important factor during those years was my fellow hostages.*

NATURAL DISASTERS

It is easier, perhaps, to find a rhyme or reason or rationale to cope with personal disaster than to try to come to terms with a natural disaster or catastrophe. The annals of history are littered with records of disasters which have cast a shadow that lingers long after those who have perished have been forgotten. Way back in the year AD 79 an estimated twenty thousand people in Pompeii were buried alive under ash and lava and fallen rooftops when the volcano Vesuvius erupted. You could argue that anyone choosing to live in the shadow of a volcano takes a calculated risk, but that is no explanation for the horror of such a calamity.

* The *Observer*, March 15th, 1992.

In my own career within the BBC, I have found myself in the Newsroom as a Foreign Duty Editor when news has come in of a catastrophe. It is always horrific and often beyond our comprehension. I wish I could conjure up an instant explanation for the disasters and horrors that so upset us. Biblically, all of this is the ultimate result of the broken relationship between us and God and between us and nature. We humans are capable of inflicting indescribable pain upon one another, as we have witnessed in the war in Bosnia and the former Yugoslavia in 1992 and 1993.

I well remember the horror of being the first to hear Mark Tully's eyewitness reports for BBC Radio of the death of thousands of people and livestock in the Bhopal gas disaster in India in 1985. The following year I was on shift when the first reports came through of an unusually high radioactivity reading in Scandinavia. That was the first the world knew of the Chernobyl nuclear reactor disaster in the Soviet Union. Disasters like this can be explained in terms of human failure. But far harder to face up to are the natural disasters – mass starvation in Ethiopia and Somalia, floods and cyclones in Bangladesh.

To some extent even these are, in theory, avoidable. We live in a world in which countries like Bangladesh have millions of people living below sea level on plains that they know will flood with the next seasonal cyclone. There is enough food to prevent starvation in Africa if the political will were there. Often starvation is the result of civil war, international debt and world trade patterns as much as lack of rain. But it is the foolish person who tries to explain all of this away in simplistic terms.

Some disasters stem directly from human folly. Others result from the forces of nature and our interaction with those same forces. It is too easy for us to blame God and deny our own collective responsibility for what happens around us. When something happens that appals us and causes us distress, we want to distance ourselves from it and pin the blame on anyone other than ourselves. In the summer of 1993 there were disastrous floods in the United States and in Bangladesh. Both were declared national disasters. But the death toll in America was relatively low and the main concern was the damage to property and to agriculture. President Clinton was quick to offer millions of dollars of federal relief. In Bangladesh, thousands died. Interestingly, as the flood waters rose in America, it was the Bangladesh government who offered to supply jute sandbags to help keep the Mississippi at bay. In Bangladesh, the main casualty of flooding is not farmland but the population itself. We are all to blame in part and each of us has a responsibility to do what we can to help.

The prophet Isaiah has the last word on the plight of our planet: 'The floodgates of the heavens are opened, the foundations of the earth shake. The earth is broken up, the earth is split asunder, the earth is thoroughly shaken. The earth reels like a drunkard, it sways like a hut in the wind; so heavy upon it is the guilt of its rebellion that it falls – never to rise again' (Isa. 24: 18–20).

THE SUFFERING OF JOB

One of those books in the Bible that surely must have struck a very deep chord in Terry Anderson's heart through that most painful seven-year ordeal is the book of Job. It has much to teach us.

Job had to get to know himself in a far more painful way as he found himself at the heart of a spiritual conflict, the scale of which he could barely imagine. From the man who had everything he became the man who had lost everything. With good reason we always identify Job with suffering and personal torment. Yet we neglect at our peril the understanding he gained through the suffering he endured. We see that, despite his suffering, he retains his absolute reliance on God. It is this which sees him through the darkest days.

Job's friends tried to explain away his suffering, seeking in his past some terrible misdeed as the cause of his troubles. Job knew better than that and trusted God. His attitude is summed up in chapter 23: 'Even today my complaint is bitter; his hand is heavy in spite of my groaning. If only I knew where to find him; if only I could go to his dwelling! I would state my case before him and fill my mouth with arguments' (Job 23: 2–4). The fact is, however, that Job's attempts to find God come to nothing: 'If I go to the east, he is not there; if I go to the west, I do not find him. When he is at work in the north, I do not see him; when he turns to the south, I catch no glimpse of him' (23: 8–9). Then Job's confidence shines through like a strong torch on a misty night: 'But he knows the way that I take; when he has tested me, I shall come forth as gold' (23: 10).

This confidence is based on Job's own personal and spiritual life. 'My feet have closely followed his steps; I have kept to his way without turning aside. I have not departed from the commands of his lips; I have treasured the words of his mouth more than my daily bread' (23: 11–12).

From this we see that Job had a clear sense of God's guiding hand in his life. Even when he was at his lowest ebb, when God was nowhere in sight and he might have had every justification in concluding that God was not there for him, we find Job's faith intact. He was able to draw upon his inner resources like a man drawing water from a deep well within. He knows he will personally come through the test because God knows him so well: 'He knows the way that I take'. Job had a proper sense of direction in his life. He knew who he was and where he had come from; he knew his current predicament. He also knew what was getting in the way and he seemed to sense how it was going to work out.

Remember how the book of Job ends – not with him bemoaning his lot and writhing in agony over his suffering. Not a bit of it. Job is restored. He acknowledges to God what he has learned. The most important lesson of all is that God cannot be thwarted and that any speculation on Job's part had been an exercise in speaking of things 'I did not understand, things too wonderful for me to know' (42: 3). God made him prosperous again and gave him twice as much as he had before. This included 14,000 sheep, 6,000 camels and 1,000 oxen, not to mention ten children and a very long life. So don't feel too sorry for poor old Job! We should not, of course, expect or assume a happy ending to a time of deep despair. Job was fortunate.

I think Job's experience can be very helpful to us. And the way in which he worked through his current state of mind is in itself a case study in maintaining your confidence in God in the face of personal loss and suffering.

MY GREATEST LOSS

Few of us will have had any experience to compare with that of Roy Castle, Terry Anderson, or Job. But all of us have to face at some moment the tragic loss of someone we love. It can deal a body blow to faith. In my own case, the greatest loss I have ever had to endure is the death of my father from cancer of the stomach. He was only fifty-six years old when he died and I was just nineteen and near the end of my first year away from home at college. He died at home, surrounded by the family and at peace with the God in whom he believed with firm conviction. Yet even the knowledge of that cannot prevent the sense of loss and dereliction that bereavement brings.

I knew that my father was ill. He had gone into hospital for an operation to deal with what doctors believed was an ulcer. What they found was not a grumbling ulcer but a stomach ravaged with cancer. We were told he had a year to live. Although I'm sure in his heart of hearts he knew he was slowly dying, he lived that last year as if he was on the road to recovery. It was on April 30th that, at the end of a perfectly normal and busy student day full of activity, I rang home at 11.45 p.m. to find out how he was. My brother told me the news that the doctors had given my father just four weeks to live. My mother sounded all right, according to the diary note I scribbled down later. I spent the next two hours coming to terms with the news. I wrote to three close friends asking for them to pray. I put on a record of Christian music and read the Bible and prayed. My diary records that I found Isaiah 40 a great comfort. At 2.40 a.m. I went to bed. Four weeks later my father died.

In our grief and sorrow as a family at my father's death, we found tremendous strength in our support for each other and, most of all, in the very real experience of God's love buoying us up like a life raft on the choppy waters of our tears. I remember listening a lot to Handel's *Messiah* and discovering afresh the depth of Paul's writings on death.

> If it is preached that Christ has been raised from the dead, how can some of you say that there is no resurrection of the dead? If there is no resurrection of the dead, then not even Christ has been raised. And if Christ has not been raised, our preaching is useless and so is your faith . . . But Christ has indeed been raised from the dead (1 Cor. 15: 12–14, 20).

He ends with a ringing and confident declaration that death has been swallowed up in victory:

> The sting of death is sin, and the power of sin is the law. But thanks be to God! He gives us the victory through our Lord Jesus Christ. Therefore, my dear brothers, stand firm. Let nothing move you. Always give yourselves fully to the work of the Lord, because you know that your labour in the Lord is not in vain (1 Cor. 15: 56–58).

I once heard a Baptist pastor, Roger Hayden, describe grief as the price we pay for love, the cost of our commitment to someone. He said that the tears and grief we go through are a part of that vital process of healing. Just as Jesus's heart went out to the widow of Nain in her grief (Luke 7: 11–17), so too we must show that same compassion to those who are grieving. He also pointed out Jesus's power to change the situation as he did with the widow's son, raising him from death. The good news is that there is triumph over death and there is recovery. 'Jesus is victor' was his message. From my own experience, Jesus can restore our confidence and our wellbeing as we go through the pain of bereavement.

Death, suffering and bereavement are powerful destroyers of Christian confidence. But they can equally become building blocks to a stronger faith that can move mountains.

7
CONFIDENCE IN CHRISTIAN ORIGINS

It was a typical week in an English summer – cold, wet and windy. A small village in Leicestershire called Wymeswold was playing host to an invasion of two thousand travelling people – gypsies as they are more often called. Normally, a gathering of this number of travellers would provoke complaints from the community and a large police presence, but not this time. The gypsies were attending a week-long Christian convention for travellers. After a week of prayer, Bible study, preaching and fellowship they moved on. According to Jackie Boyd of the Gypsies and Travellers' Evangelical Movement, out of an estimated sixty thousand travellers in Britain, five thousand are Christians. In France there are now an estimated eighty thousand Christian gypsies and in Spain the figure is nearer one hundred thousand. 'Now we go up and down the country and wherever we go, we go to church every Sunday and people accept us – when people don't I feel sorry for them,' says Jackie Boyd in an article in the *Observer*, August 1st, 1993. 'Non-gypsies didn't tell the gypsies about Jesus Christ, they were too frightened. It took the French gypsies to tell the English gypsies.'

It was talking about Jesus Christ that made the difference. The French travellers clearly did not hold back from talking about their faith in Jesus. They did so with confidence, sure of what they believed and willing to export their discovery to Britain. They succeeded where ordinary British Christians had failed through fear, if Jackie Boyd is right. Too many of us, it seems, are either unsure of or simply do not know some of the basic facts of our own faith.

Not everyone is interested in history or finds it easy to

read the Bible. Many of us are content to let others do the homework or come up with the answers to such tricky questions as, 'How can we be sure that Jesus really died on the Cross?' or, 'Isn't the Resurrection just wishful thinking or fantasy?' When faced with a direct question ourselves, we can all too easily stumble over something for which there is probably a simple answer, but which we don't have readily to hand. The purpose of this chapter is to spell out simply some of the basic facts about the Christian faith. If we are to be confident in our faith we must have confidence that our faith is based on fact and not on fantasy.

THE FIRST-CENTURY WORLD

Let's be clear about the context into which Jesus was born. To some extent every generation likes to reinterpret Jesus in its own mould. There is perhaps one strand of Jesus's teaching or character that carries a special resonance. In the 1960s the 'flower culture' turned Jesus into a hippie figure and teenage Christians started to call themselves 'Jesus People'. In the 1970s it was 'Jesus Christ Superstar' who held mass appeal. In the 1980s Jesus the Healer became the contemporary image and in the 1990s it is the mystical and spiritual side of Jesus that rings true. When we look at the figure of Jesus, there are always many layers of interpretation added on, and we must cut through these to get to the real Jesus of history. Jesus's personality is so magnetic and his teaching so compelling, that he has always been and still is a subject of fascination and enquiry.

Some interpreters of Jesus's life find it convenient to try to draw a hard and fast line between the Jesus of history and the Christ of faith. Many a modern biographer of Jesus has claimed that we have to set to one side the Christian doctrines about Jesus's identity and try to get back to the bare facts of the Jesus of history. But it is a false distinction they make. We rely so much on the Gospel records that you cannot just take a pair of scissors and cut out bits that don't conveniently fit the latest theory. We have to ask if the Gospels are a reliable source. To assess that, it helps if we can picture the world into which Jesus was born.

THE BACKDROP

Jesus was born into a world dominated by Rome. Just as in our day, American influence spreads far and wide and its military power can be exercised far away from base, so too the power of Rome was felt even in far off Palestine. During the fifty years before Jesus was born, Julius Caesar was murdered in 44 BC and his great-nephew beat Mark Anthony at Actium in 31 BC. So began the *Pax Romana* of Augustus Caesar, a period of peace and prosperity for the Empire. Augustus died in AD 14. A network of new roads united the civilised world and communications were better than ever before. The time was ripe for God to intervene in human events. Among the Jews expectation of the imminent arrival of a Messiah was rising. Scattered groups of Jews in strategic centres around the Empire provided the apostle Paul with a ready-made audience for the good news he was to bring of the Messiah's arrival.

Palestine was an occupied country with a strong resistance movement led by Nationalists who hoped for a political Messiah to lead them into military victory over the Roman occupying forces. The Zealots refused to pay taxes to Rome. The high priests and the Sadducees collaborated with Rome. Into this turbulent atmosphere Jesus was born.

SOURCES FOR THE LIFE OF JESUS

It is a mistake to think that the Gospels are the only sources for information about Jesus. They are not. I should say straight away that no historian seriously questions that Jesus did exist as a historical figure. Quite apart from the Gospels, there are pagan and Jewish historical sources that point to the existence of Jesus as a real person who lived and died. There is also ample archaeological evidence to testify to his reality.

In fact, on documentary evidence alone, if you include the New Testament writings, it is easier to find writings about Jesus than about Julius Caesar. If you exclude them, there is still more than enough convincing evidence that Jesus was a flesh and blood person who lived in space and time.

Who would ever have heard of Pontius Pilate if it was not for the story of Jesus? If you visit the ancient Roman port of Caesarea Maritima, now in northern Israel, a stone inscribed with Pilate's name, 'Pontious Pilate, Praefectus Judaea', was discovered during excavations. You can see a copy of it in Caesarea today, as I have myself, or examine the original in the Rockefeller Museum in Jerusalem.

A carpenter-teacher in a frontier province of Rome would not attract much attention from Roman historians except in so far as he caused difficulties for the Empire. Therefore it is not surprising that Jesus did not arouse much interest. None the less we find Pliny the Younger, who was sent by Trajan to northern Turkey in AD 112, writing that pagan temples were closing and Christians were refusing to worship the Emperor. He records that they met on a certain day, sang a hymn to Christ as God, took oaths not to commit crime and ate a common meal (Pliny, *Epistles*, 10. 96).

Tacitus, greatest historian of imperial Rome, wrote: 'The name Christian comes to them from Christ who was executed in the reign of Tiberius by the Procurator Pontius Pilate. The pernicious superstition, suppressed for a while, broke out afresh and spread not only through Judaea the source of the malady but even through Rome itself' (Tacitus, *Annals*, 15. 44, quoted by Michael Green, *Runaway World*, IVP, 1968, p. 13).

Tacitus and Pliny both agree Jesus existed. Writing even earlier, in AD 52 Thallus, who was a Samaritan-born historian, suggests an eclipse caused the darkness at Calvary when Jesus was executed. Another writer, Julius Africanus, questions this. We find the circumstances of Jesus's death well known in Rome, even to pagan historians.

Suetonius (AD 69–140) says that Claudius expelled Jews from Rome in AD 49 because of riots instigated on behalf of 'Chrestus'.

JOSEPHUS FLAVIUS

The most important non-Christian source is the Jewish historian Josephus Flavius. At the beginning of the great Jewish revolt of AD 66, Josephus Flavius was one of the Jewish commanders in Galilee. Later he went over to the Romans. Because of this switch of allegiance, Jewish historians were sceptical of him as a reliable source. His description of the Jewish War and of what took place on the summit of Masada in the spring of AD 73 is very detailed and utterly compelling – so much so that, until the expeditions took place in the 1960s, many dismissed his accounts as fanciful. Then Yigael Yadin led an archaeological team to excavate the hilltop fortress of Masada, at the eastern edge of the Judean desert.

The Rock of Masada has a 1,300 foot drop to the western shore of the Dead Sea, a place of stark beauty. I was fortunate to be able to see it for myself in April 1992 and it is a fascinating place. It is remarkable how much has been preserved in the dry, sandy climate. When you look at Herod the Great's private bathroom at Masada, you can see not only the plumbing system and the mosaic flooring, but much of the tiling and decoration have also survived two thousand years, and many of the bath tiles survive to this day.

Palestine was under Roman occupation and from time to time there were rebellions. The most serious was the Jewish revolt of AD 66, which flared up into a four-year civil war. In AD 70 the Roman General Titus conquered Jerusalem, destroyed the Temple and expelled the surviving Jews. One outpost held out until AD 73 after taking refuge in Herod's fortress and palace at Masada. In AD 72 the Roman Governor marched on Masada determined to crush the final resistance. The Jews prepared their defences and set up water systems to help them survive what was to be a very long siege. The Romans broke the siege by building a ramp of beaten earth, on which they built a siege tower to breach the fortress wall. That night, the leader of the Zealots inside Masada knew there was no escape and no hope of relief. It was death or surrender.

Rather than be taken into slavery by the Romans, the defenders – 960 men, women and children – took their own lives. When the Romans reached the top of the fortress the next day, Josephus Flavius tells us they were met with silence. 'And so met the Romans with the multitude of the slain, but could take no pleasure in the fact, though it were done to their enemies. Nor could they do other than wonder at the courage of their resolution and at the immoveable contempt of death which so great a number of them had shown, when they went through such an action as this.'[*]

No wonder that Masada has remained a symbol of Jewish resistance to this day and has made heroes of the Zealots who died there. But what of Josephus Flavius? The two expeditions of 1963 and 1964 ended up by confirming the detailed accuracy of Josephus Flavius as a historian and chronicler of events. What had been questioned by scholars as fanciful writing to enhance the story turned out, on closer examination, to be an accurate description of what had taken place. As one example, Josephus in *The Jewish War* says that, years before Herod fortified Masada, the site had been used as a refuge by Herod's brother Joseph. He recalls one incident in which those taking refuge were about to die of thirst when suddenly the heavens opened and all the pits filled with water, saving their lives. This report from Josephus has seemed too far-fetched, but, in the words of the archaeologist Yigael Yadin:

> This report in Josephus had been hard to believe; for even if one could imagine the waters of the wadis piling up to fill the cisterns from the rains of Masada – or more particularly from the westward flowing rain-water of the Judean hills – it was difficult to conceive that direct rain over the Masada summit would be enough to fill its clefts. Yet I recall one of those days when we all had to rush for shelter from a sudden downpour. When it was over, I was astonished to behold that the low-lying areas of the summit were now one huge pool of water. If I had not myself photographed this

---

[*] Yigael Yadin, *Masada*, Weidenfeld and Nicholson, 1962, p. 12. For a full account of the siege of Masada, see Josephus Flavius, *The Jewish War*, Penguin Classics, revised edition 1981, pp. 395–405.

Confidence in Christian Origins

sight, I would not have believed that it had been taken at the top of Masada. So this story of Josephus had evidently also been based on reliable information.*

Josephus Flavius wrote *The Jewish War* between AD 70 and AD 75 and two decades later he wrote his *Jewish Antiquities*. This includes a very specific passage about Jesus. When you read this, it is important to remember that Josephus Flavius was a Jewish historian and not a Christian. There is no reason whatever for him to write sympathetically about Jesus. Yet his *Antiquities* includes this passage.

> And there arose about this time Jesus, a wise man, if indeed he should be called a man. For he was a doer of marvellous deeds, and was a teacher of such people as are eager for novelties. He attracted many Jews and many of the Greeks. This man was the Messiah. And when Pilate had condemned him to the cross at the instigation of our own leaders, those who had loved him from the first did not cease to do so. For he appeared to them on the third day alive again, as the holy prophets had predicted and said many other wonderful things about him. And even now the tribe of Christians named after him is not extinct. (*Antiquities*, 18. 3. 3)

This is such strong evidence, from a non-Christian and unsympathetic source, that Jesus did exist, was crucified by the Romans and appeared alive on the third day to Christians, that inevitably it has brought controversy. With so little about Jesus in *The Jewish War* but so much in his *Antiquities* twenty years later, can Josephus Flavius be trusted? In fact there is no reason not to trust him. Josephus Flavius' account can be trusted for four reasons.

First, Josephus Flavius' details about Masada have been questioned too, but have stood up to the closest archaeological tests of our day. If he can be trusted on minor details of Masada's plumbing systems, surely he can be trusted to

---

* Yigael Yadin, *Masada*, p. 34.

know the basic facts about the leader of a schismatic sect of great nuisance to his masters, the Romans.

Secondly, in the context in which this passage occurs, Josephus Flavius is more interested in James, the leader of the early church, than in Jesus. Why bother to mention Jesus at all, unless James was a member of this group to whom Josephus Flavius attached such importance – the early church?

Thirdly, and here I refer to Mary Smallwood's comments in the 1981 revised Penguin Classic edition of *The Jewish War*: 'Not only for the war of 66–70 but also for the history of the province of Judaea, and for the story of the reigns of Herod the Great, his sons and his grandson, Josephus stands virtually alone, and must be judged on his own merits' (p. 19).

Finally, we know that the fourth-century historian Eusebius read the passage in his copy of Josephus and quotes it twice, even if once he is doing so with tongue firmly in cheek with phrases like 'if indeed we should call him a man'.*

What we have here in Josephus Flavius is an important early manuscript and, from an independent source with no Christian axe to grind, we find powerful evidence of the existence of the early church. It gives one historian's account, from a non-Christian perspective, of the origins of that church, for which the writer has no personal allegiance. Given that Josephus Flavius was a Jewish renegade who had switched allegiance to Rome, the fact that he writes with such detachment about Jesus makes it all the more powerful as evidence.

Josephus' reputation has taken on a whole new lease of life since the Jewish excavations in the hilltop fortress of Masada. His detailed descriptions of what took place have been corroborated and shown to be remarkably accurate by archaeological excavation. As a result, his reputation as a historian and a stickler for accurate detail has been enhanced. So why should he be applauded for one account and discounted for another? If Josephus Flavius is an ancient recorder to be

---

* Michael Green, *Runaway World*, Intervarsity Press, 1968.

Confidence in Christian Origins 163

trusted with a true history of the siege of Masada, then why not an account of the origins of Christianity which, after all, precede the events at Masada?

ARCHAEOLOGICAL REMAINS

Even if we were to discount the Gospels from our calculations, we find that the evidence for the documentary existence of Jesus Christ and the early church is convincing and compelling. We can draw confidence from this. But when we begin to look at the archaeological remains, the picture is more exciting still. We are fortunate that the modern state of Israel takes archaeology very seriously and has made significant progress in uncovering Jewish, Roman and Christian remains. The fact is that the more they dig, the closer we get to our origins and the more we find to strengthen our faith and to encourage us.

Any visitor to Israel today is faced with an increasing body of evidence that validates what we read and find in Scripture, both Old and New Testaments. Some of that evidence is quite breathtaking. For example, we read in the Gospels of how Jesus predicts the destruction of Jerusalem. It was always believed that these prophecies were fulfilled when the Romans sacked Jerusalem in AD 70. But it was only after the Six Day War in 1967 that the most telling evidence came to light.

In that war, Jordanian aircraft had flattened the Jewish quarter of old Jerusalem. In clearing away the rubble, it was discovered that a whole new layer of the city's past had been uncovered by the bombing. The archaeologists got to work. What they found can now be seen in the magnificent Wohl Archaeological Museum in the Herodian Quarter.

Here there is a room where a ferocious fire has raged and brought down the ceiling. Charred cypress beams lie on the mosaic floor and the edge of the mosaic flooring is also charred and discoloured. The fire swept through the adjoining room and all along two other excavated buildings. In case there is any doubt remaining that this is physical evidence of the great conflagration which destroyed Jerusalem, under the mosaic floor a coin from Herod's era was discovered. Its date is AD 70, the year Jerusalem was destroyed.

THE SOUTHERN STEPS

Since the beginning of the excavations in 1968, many tons of rubble have been removed, Ivory and bronze figures and coins from different periods have been found and earlier structures uncovered for the first time. Excavations have revealed the remains of an enormous right-angled stairway leading to the Temple Mount from the south. The uppermost arch is still visible, jutting out of the Western Wall near its southern corner and named 'Robinson's Arch' after the explorer who discovered it. Of most interest to Christians is the discovery of the southern steps to the main gates of the Temple. If you sit on these steps today – in itself an extraordinary experience – you sit where Jesus himself sat.

It is one of the few Christian sites in Jerusalem of which there can be no doubt about its authenticity. As you sit there you look across to the white tombs on the Mount of Olives, where the bodies of the great and the good are buried. The words of Jesus ring out as he sat on those steps and condemned the religious leaders of the day: 'You hypocrites! You are like whitewashed tombs, which look beautiful on the outside but on the inside are full of dead men's bones and everything unclean' (Matt. 23: 27). The words take on a new vividness and potency when today you can still see what is, in effect, the identical view Jesus had so long ago. His illustrations were taken from life, not as we know it today, but still as we can see it.

It is hard to believe but, despite the fact that death by crucifixion was common in first-century Palestine and used by the Romans all across their Empire to punish opponents (including those involved in the revolt led by the slave Spartacus), no archaeological proof of crucifixion by nails was found until 1968. This was a human heel-bone of a man crucified two thousand years ago and it can be seen

Confidence in Christian Origins 165

in Jerusalem's Department of Antiquity. The nail is bent, evidence of what Josephus Flavius described as crucifixion by a 'cruel and novel' manner used against Jewish Zealots.

THE POMPEII RIDDLE

My Uncle Humphrey loves crosswords. He will happily spend hours wrestling with a clue to find the right word. When he does it in collaboration with my mother, they are a lethal combination. One of the most intriguing archaeological puzzles is one which will appeal to all crossword freaks like my uncle. It occurs scattered across the Roman Empire from Dura Europos on the Euphrates at the eastern fringe to Manchester in Britain near the northern frontier. It is an acrostic inscription, found also in Pompeii, which hides a riddle. It is a Latin word square, which reads the same in every direction, horizontally and vertically. This is what was found:

```
R O T A S
O P E R A
T E N E T
A R E P O
S A T O R
```

The translation is 'The sower Arepo holds the wheels with care'. It doesn't seem to make any sense as a saying – who cares how the sower holds the wheels? But what if this is some secret code, a message hidden in a riddle? If you rearrange the letters, a possible solution emerges. Regrettably, though many samples of the riddle have survived the ravages of time, we can only offer an intelligent guess at the solution. But by far the most convincing is that the riddle is a secret Christian affirmation of faith, cunningly disguised. If you rearrange the letters, you end up with this Cross-shaped creed:

```
                A

                P

                A

                T

                E

                R

    A PATERNOSTER O

                O

                S

                T

                E

                R

                O
```

What is its hidden meaning? The letters add up to a repeated prayer – the *Pater Noster* (Our Father) – plus 'A' and 'O' twice – Jesus as Alpha and Omega, the beginning and the end (see Rev. 1:8).

The address to God as Father echoes the words Jesus taught the disciples (Matt. 6: 9 ff). The cruciform shape shows the centrality of the Cross of Jesus – quite as extraordinary as if a modern group chose the gallows for a symbol. The Alpha and Omega express belief in Jesus as of ultimate significance. The word 'tenet' in the middle of the original word square means 'he holds' and is itself a statement of faith at a time when Christians were being persecuted by Nero. This was the basis of faith – that Jesus could hold them even when facing death, an assurance based on historical roots.

THE CATACOMBS

Any visitor to the Catacombs in Rome – the secret burial chambers of the first Christians – will see that the symbol used to show a Christian grave was not the Cross but a fish or an anchor. As we have discussed earlier, the fish is still worn today as a Christian symbol of the Greek word for fish which is 'ICHTHUS' (see p. 60).

This is more evidence of what the first generation of Christians believed – that Jesus Christ is not just another man but is God's own Son and the Saviour who came to save us from ourselves and to bring us back to God. We can draw confidence ourselves from this assured statement of faith from Christians who died so long ago.

The Catacombs are rich in Christian symbols. Some like the fish, dove and anchor are familar to Christians today; others are less so. In the burial chambers of the Christians of Rome, the so-called Catacombs of St Callixtus, you can see other Christian symbols, long forgotten. They include the hare, used as an image of the believer who fears the snares of evil and seeks refuge. There is the palm and the crown, symbolising Christian martyrs who have shed their blood for their faith and are now with God in glory, with palm branches in their hands (see Rev. 7: 9ff. for a fuller reference to the palm symbol). Another lost Christian symbol is the cock, herald of the new day and the light of dawn, an invitation to praise God as opposed to the night with its darkness of evil.* Symbols were used both as secret signs and as visual aids. They are vibrant with a faith that is sure and brings us close to Christians for whom the price of faith was often public execution.

PONTIUS PILATE FOUND IN CAESAREA

In the year 20 BC Herod the Great rebuilt the town of Caesarea along the Mediterranean coast. It was occupied by the Crusaders from western Europe in 1102 but by 1291 it had been destroyed. The city was abandoned and gradually buried under sand dunes. In 1956 archaeologists began excavating Caesarea, unearthing such important remains as the Roman amphitheatre and the aqueduct which brought water to the

---

* Antonia Baruffa, *The Catacombs of St Callixtus*, LEV, Vatican City, third edition 1992, pp. 38–9.

city from the mountains twelve miles away. Archaeologists also found a stone tablet inscribed with the name of Pontius Pilate. This is the first archaeological evidence of the famous Roman procurator who condemned Jesus to the Cross.*

ARE THE GOSPELS RELIABLE?

Whatever accumulated evidence we can put together from pagan writers and from archaeological remains, we come back to the Gospels of Matthew, Mark, Luke and John as our prime source material for the life of Jesus. If we are to use them as our main source of information about Jesus, it helps if we can be confident that they are reliable. Can we be confident that the Gospels themselves are to be trusted as reliable history and not a later invention of fertile minds anxious to prove a point?

In my opinion, they can be trusted and I'll explain why. It's a common mistake to think of the Gospels as some kind of first-century biography. They are not. What they don't tell us exceeds what they do tell us.

The Gospels are a record of Jesus's three years of ministry. They tell us more about his last week than they do about his first thirty years. As biographies they are a hopeless failure. They tell us next to nothing of his childhood. They tell us in great detail what his enemies thought of him, which is more honest and courageous than most biographers are when writing about someone they revere. The Gospel writers don't even tell us what he looked like. The Gospels, however, were not intended as biographies: they are a different kind of record of Jesus's life, written for very specific reasons.

THE GOSPELS' DIRECTIVE

Why were they written at all? And why apparently so late? After all, it was thirty or forty years after Jesus died before

---

* Sami Awwad, *The Holy Land*, Palphot Ltd, 1992, p. 117.

they were written, and the first Gospel to be put down in writing was not even by one of the twelve disciples, but by Mark. The Roman historian Papias tells us that Mark was with the fisherman-turned-disciple Peter when he was in prison in Rome awaiting death at Nero's hand. Mark wrote down all that Peter remembered. Not surprisingly, therefore, there is no account of Jesus's birth in Mark's Gospel. Peter would have had no interest in that. Most of Mark's writings are reproduced in the Gospels of Matthew and Luke, so that further suggests that Mark came first.

Why, then, was there such an interval between Jesus's death and the Gospels being written down? Can we be confident that the Gospel accounts are accurate and trustworthy?

A first point to remember is that there was no need to record a written life while those who heard and knew Jesus were still alive. Put crudely, you don't need to read John's Gospel if John is preaching at your local congregation the following Sunday. It was only as those who had seen and heard Jesus began to grow old that the need to get their recollections written down became urgent.

Secondly, remember the culture of the day. Jewish Rabbis were extremely careful to hand down oral material accurately and we can assume that Christians felt the same way about Jesus's teaching. The Gospel material was originally taught in Aramaic, the language spoken by Jesus, and in a poetic form easy to memorise. But the Gospels were written in Greek, though many Aramaic words survive to confirm the authentic origins. Oral tradition would have ensured that Jesus's teaching was memorised word by word and passed on from father to son.

THE ACCURACY OF ORAL TRADITION

What is more, the language of Jesus survives to this day and so does oral tradition, with the help of audio cassettes. It is a linguistic mystery of our times that Aramaic has survived amongst the eighteen thousand inhabitants of Maaloula and two nearby Syrian villages, Bakhaa and Joubadeen. A newspaper correspondent from *The Times* tracked down the senior clergyman at the local Greek Orthodox church. 'It is truly amazing,' said the priest, 'when you see a baby being spoken to in Aramaic, you are immediately transported back to what it must have been like when the baby Jesus was addressed by Mary.'

The priest plays a tape of the Lord's Prayer in Aramaic to visitors and pilgrims. How the use of Aramaic survived as a language, when it was believed to have died out when the Arabs conquered the region, has remained a mystery. The Syrians use it in their homes; they speak it, but they do not read or write it. The most likely theory is that the people were transported there from elsewhere and have preserved the tongue through oral tradition alone for well over one thousand years. A local shop assistant told *The Times* correspondent: 'We are all very proud to speak the same language that Christ himself spoke. At home and in the street, we use it all the time' (*The Times*, January 26th, 1993).

If Aramaic has survived until the present day – albeit only in one Syrian town and two villages – through oral tradition alone, then we see how powerful that tradition is. So we can begin to comprehend how Jesus's teaching survived intact by word of mouth until the time came for it to be written down.

It is true that people remember what they want to remember, but this does not mean that Jesus's hearers forgot what they found disturbing. The Gospels are full of hard sayings – challenging and difficult teachings, carefully preserved. For example, Jesus saying that any man who looks at a woman lustfully has committed adultery with her in his heart, or that you should love your enemies and pray for those who persecute you, is hardly heart-warming stuff.

We are not dealing with a sophisticated culture here, but one where few could read and where stories were passed on from parent to child, learned by heart and retold without alteration or adjustment. The reliability of the oral tradition is backed by what some see as contradictions in the Gospel accounts. In fact most of these apparent contradictions reflect differences in the purposes of the Gospel writers, or differences in the calendars they used – Gregorian or Julian.

THE NEED FOR AN ACCURATE RECORD

The story of Jesus was remembered and recalled because it was relevant to the life of the Church. For example, faced with arguments from the Jews, it was important that Christians remembered how Jesus debated with them. It was essential to remember which Old Testament passages Jesus read aloud when he preached in the synagogue, because those passages gave clues about how Jesus saw himself. Matthew is especially keen to show how Jesus fulfilled the expectations Jews had of the Chosen One, the Messiah. Luke often draws on the writings of the prophet Isaiah to show Jesus as God's Servant who was to suffer and die, just as Isaiah 53 had prophesied.

Faced with ethical decisions such as marriage and divorce, they needed Jesus's teaching as the final authority on such matters. So just as the Bible has become for Christians the supreme authority in matters of faith and conduct, so Jesus's teaching was for the first Christians who had no written New Testament. When you read the Gospels you have to ask yourself: Why has the Gospel writer included this? What significance did it have for the early church? In this way the Gospels are not academic histories or simple biographies, they are practical handbooks for first-century Christians.

Scholars recognise that, whatever the different treatment given to the source materials available to them, the Gospel writers are describing one and the same Jesus Christ. All four Gospels build on historical tradition.

We must be careful not to apply twentieth-century standards here. After all, every week new biographies come out of people dead and gone. Is anyone suggesting, for example, that Peter Ackroyd's biography of Charles Dickens is any less reliable because it's been written a century after Dickens' death? In fact the reverse is true. Even in the ancient world you find long gaps between the writers putting pen to paper and the events they describe. Biographers use available sources to best advantage. So did the Gospel writers. That's why Luke, whose special interest was the universal nature of Jesus's teaching, is the only Gospel writer to include such important parables as the Prodigal Son and the Good Samaritan. He went to Caesarea, heard the stories and included them in his Gospel. If he had not, we would never know them. The Gospel writers do not give an exhaustive or comprehensive account of Jesus's life. It is a selective one. None the less, they contain all you need to know, the essential information.

'Gospel' means 'Good News' and that was their purpose – to be the carriers of the good news about Jesus; the good news that, in John's phrase, God has taken on human flesh and is pleased to dwell in our midst: not as a half-caste God-man but as a 100 per cent human being showing 100 per cent of God's attributes and character.

Not everyone will see it as good news. I had a schoolfriend called Tony who was interested in Christianity. He read the Gospels and he read a book about the Resurrection. At the end of it he was convinced that Christianity was true, that Jesus did live and die and that he was resurrected. But Tony liked his life the way it was and did not want to become a Christian. In his head he was convinced, but his heart was not in it. Whether or not he ever became a Christian I have no idea; we lost touch. Every person has to make up their own mind and God does call people in his own time, not in ours. All I could do was to respect Tony's decision and to hope and pray that his intellectual assent to the truth of the gospel would one day lead him to a personal commitment to Christ.

I have tried to explain that the Gospels rest on reliable tradition, handed down with care in the Church. At the same time they aim to show the significance of Jesus's life, in order to persuade us, the readers, that this same Jesus is no ordinary man. So they are more than just historical records: the Gospel writers reflect their own interests. But the same writers go out of their way to tell us that we can trust what they say.

Luke, who wrote the book of Acts as well as the third Gospel, starts his Gospel by saying, 'Many have undertaken to draw up an account of the things that have been fulfilled among us, just as they were handed down to us by those who from the first were eye-witnesses and servants of the word' (Luke 1: 1–2). He is keen to declare his own role: 'Therefore, since I myself have carefully investigated everything from the beginning, it seemed good also to me to write an orderly account' (1: 3).

The writer of the fourth Gospel, John, ends it with some of the most tantalising words in Scripture: 'This is the disciple who testifies to these things and who wrote them down. We know that his testimony is true. Jesus did many other things as well. If every one of them were written down, I suppose that even the whole world would not have room for the books that would be written' (John 21: 24–25). Remember that even if the fourth Gospel was the last to be written, as most scholars believe, and not written till the latter part of the first century, even then there were still eye-witnesses to these events still alive to contradict anything in the record that was untrue. No record has survived to suggest there were counter-gospel accounts written.

The Gospel writers make much of authentic eye-witness testimony and it was not in the interests of them or the Church to include anything which was not. Authenticity not fabrication is the hallmark and house style of the Gospels. The evangelists are writers, not copy typists dealing with dictation by God into some cosmic answer-phone. The Gospels were written by Christian believers to persuade people to believe, but they are none the less historical. Each writer presents Jesus in his own characteristic way.

Matthew shows how Jesus fulfilled the hopes and aspirations of the Jews for a Messiah: not a military leader, but a bringer of God's new world order into human lives – a kingdom based on God's rule in each individual's life. He shows how Jesus relates to the Jewish faith. Jews are called to see Jesus as the Messiah promised of old, the descendant of King David. Their failure to recognise Jesus as such is condemned.

Mark is more interested in action than in teaching. He stresses the responsibilities on those who follow Jesus. Mark, as I have said, is really Peter's Gospel, and like its prime source is punchy, forthright and factual. It is short on emotion but long on detail. It is Mark who introduces the idea of Jesus dying as a representative in our place (see Mark 10: 45).

Luke's interests are in the fate of non-Jews. He stresses that Jesus has come to bring people back to God. He identifies Jesus closely with the suffering servant figure, one who has come to save people from their own follies and waywardness. Jesus is a healer, he preaches to the poor and needy. To Luke, Jesus is the liberator who has time for greedy tax collectors and sinful women. Jesus shows grace – unselfish love that is born of God and that we do not deserve.

John reveals Jesus as sent by God the Father into the world – one who is the way to God, who is the truth about God and who offers a quality of life that is rich, full and abundant. For John there is ultimate significance in the life of Jesus. It is in itself life-giving. Here we find, perhaps, the best one-line description of Jesus's personality in the very first chapter: 'We have seen his glory . . . full of grace and truth' (John 1: 14).

John has taken a fair amount of stick from theologians over the years for writing later than the rest and for incorporating, according to some scholars, ideas and thinking that represent a later period. To support the idea that the fourth Gospel was written so late after the events it describes as to be next to useless as history, the Gospel's critics point to apparent archaeological inaccuracies. Matthew Arnold's book *God and the Bible*, written in 1875, is typical. He says: 'When St John wants a name for a locality, he takes the first village that comes into his remembrance, without troubling himself whether it suits or no' (p. 144).

The fact of the matter is that all the archaeology carried out in the last century has vindicated John's reputation and forced theologians to rethink and place John far earlier than previously thought. John has emerged with his reputation not only restored but enhanced. The classic case was the

Pool of Bethesda where, as told in John 5, Jesus healed the invalid. For a hundred years, this was considered an invention of John, because the pool had never been located. To make matters worse, different manuscripts used different names, among them Bethzatha, Belzetha and Bethsaida. All this changed when excavations in Jerusalem on a site north of the Temple, completed in 1932, laid bare a long lost set of two quadrilateral pools covering a wide area, with the upper pool separated from the lower pool by a wall of rock forming a gangway between them. To confirm this, the Copper Scroll from the Dead Sea Scrolls of Qumran independently confirms the existence of the double pool.

Another startling example is John's reference to Pilate judging Jesus at a place called the Pavement. This paved court was in the Governor's headquarters, but where was it? Well, any visitor to Jerusalem can now walk on a Pavement deep in the Antonia Fortress. You can see a paving stone with a Roman game marked upon it. Although this probably lies above the original Pavement, the existence of such an area as described by John again points to his reliability as a witness. If you want to read more, there are many similar examples given in A. M. Hunter's book *According to John* (SCM Press, 1968).

WHAT WAS JESUS LIKE?

The circumstances of Jesus's birth have been clouded for us by all the sentimental pap of the Victorian Christmas cards. Matthew tells us of the shepherds and Luke of the overseas visitors – the three wise men – though that is not a biblical expression. The point is this: Jesus's physical birth was utterly ordinary, in fact rather unpleasant. He was born in an animal shelter, probably a cave rather than at a wayside tavern, but certainly in very humble circumstances. His conception was anything but ordinary: born to a Jewish girl betrothed to a carpenter; conceived by God, the only supernatural ingredient in the birth. Unless you include the star of Bethlehem, to which astronomer Patrick Moore once devoted a feature in his BBC television programme *The Sky at Night*, suggesting that the planets Jupiter and Saturn were in conjunction, producing an object of staggering brightness. The dates work out too, but as Patrick Moore himself often says, 'We just do not know'.

Jesus was the son of Mary, born at Bethlehem shortly before the death of Herod the Great in 4 BC. Herod heard talk of the birth of a king and ordered the murder of all baby boys. To escape this most terrible crime, Mary and Joseph fled to Egypt and they did not return until Herod was dead and the threat passed.

Jesus's upbringing was orthodox and Jewish. Luke tells us how he was circumcised and named Jesus. There Simeon took Jesus's parents by surprise by bursting into spontaneous praise of God (Luke 2: 29), describing this eight-day-old baby as a 'light for revelation to the Gentiles and for glory to your people Israel'. When Joseph and Mary had done everything required of them by the Jewish traditions they returned to Galilee, to Nazareth where Jesus was brought up. Luke tells us the child grew and became strong – he was filled with wisdom and the grace of God was upon him. We know nothing more until Jesus is twelve years old. At that age his parents took him to Jerusalem, but somehow managed to leave without him on the way back!

When they couldn't find him amongst relatives and friends – suggesting again Jesus was brought up amongst a large, extended family – they went back to look for him. Where do they find him? Holding his own in the Temple, discussing finer theological points and asking lots of questions. 'Everyone who heard him was amazed at his understanding and his answers' (Luke 2: 47). Luke saves a different adjective for his parents' reply. Not quite apologetic but not far short of it! 'Astonished' is Luke's word. His mother says to him: '"Son, why have you treated us like this?"' Jesus's answer is so bold as to border on the precocious. '"Didn't you know I had to be in my Father's house?"' They didn't understand, but Luke tells us that Mary 'treasured all these things in her heart. And Jesus grew in wisdom and stature, and in favour with God and men' (2: 51–52).

After his birth he spent his early life in Nazareth, where he worked as the village carpenter. Although Mary continues to feature strongly in the Gospels, and was present at Jesus's death by crucifixion, Joseph disappears from the narrative altogether. It is reasonable to assume that Joseph died during Jesus's childhood – sometime after his visit to Jerusalem at the age of twelve. So Jesus knew what it was to lose his father – suffering and tragedy were no strangers to him. His mother occupied a special place in his life. One of his last acts on the Cross was to ask his closest disciple, John, to look after Mary as if she were John's own mother.

Knowing what Jesus himself experienced in his early years increases our confidence in him. He has gone through the pain of bereavement. He has suffered the loss of someone he loved very much: not only his father either, but also his best friend Lazarus, after whose death 'Jesus wept' (John 11: 35). We can feel closer to Jesus when we remember that he was an ordinary person as well an extraordinary one, in the ultimate Christian paradox of God becoming a man. This is a Jesus to whom we can relate, with whom we can share our secrets and to whom we can bring our hopes and fears in prayer. We can be confident in him because he has gone before us and experienced the lows of life as well as the high points.

JESUS'S APPEARANCE

Here we can only guess. We have been presented over the years with a visual image of Jesus by artists and film-makers that is probably inaccurate. To see Jesus in your mind's eye as a tall, athletic-looking Viking with piercing blue eyes, or as a cultured Englishman, as portrayed by Robert Powell in Zeffirelli's epic *Jesus of Nazareth* is probably wrong! He was a Palestinian Jew and therefore probably dark in complexion with brown eyes and dark hair. The closest physical image from the cinema is probably the *Gospel According to Saint Matthew*. Jesus was probably clean-shaven as well, which is how all the earliest mosaics show him. The Gospels tell us he was strong and it is clear from the authority with which he spoke and the attention he received, that he had great personal charisma – in the proper sense of the word – filled with God's grace. But he was not meek and mild. He was meek and mild when receiving small children, perhaps, but far from it when throwing the financial wheeler-dealers out of the Temple or when condemning the ultra-religious Pharisees as a brood of vipers.

JESUS'S FAMILY

Although the Gospel writers skate over the fact, Jesus was one of a large family. When Jesus preached in his home synagogue there was a similar reaction. Mark records this exchange: '"Where did this man get these things?" they asked. "What's this wisdom that has been given him, that he even does miracles! Isn't this the carpenter? Isn't this Mary's son and the brother of James, Joseph, Judas and Simon? Aren't his sisters here with us?"' (Mark 6: 2–3). So we know that Jesus had four brothers and an unnamed number of sisters.

Moreover, his brothers and sisters didn't take to him much on the whole. Jesus went around in Galilee, and I quote,

> purposely staying away from Judea because the Jews there were waiting to take his life . . . Jesus' brothers said to him, 'You ought to leave here and go to Judea, so that your disciples may see the miracles you do. No-one who wants to become a public figure acts in secret. Since you are doing these things, show yourself to the world.' For even his own brothers did not believe in him (John 7: 1–5).

One of these brothers, many believe, turns out to be a key leader of the early church: James, author of the epistle of James, the one which says 'faith without deeds is dead' (Jas. 2: 26). Though we cannot be absolutely certain that James was Jesus's brother, it looks the most likely explanation. If they are one and the same, James stands out in his letter as

Confidence in Christian Origins

being ever practical, like his brother Jesus the carpenter's son. What transformed James from cynical brother to a pillar of the early church? The only explanation offered in the Bible comes in a long list in 1 Corinthians 15 of those to whom the risen Christ appeared. The list includes James, brother of Jesus.

This isn't the place to run through the events of Jesus's life, but if we are to have confidence in the Christian faith there remain two questions that must be addressed: Why did Jesus die? Does the Resurrection – the claim that Jesus rose from the dead – stand up to scrutiny, or is it nonsense?

WHY DID JESUS DIE?

Many volumes have been written about why Jesus died. The simple answer given by Peter to the next generation is this: he died to bring us to God. Jesus died, if you like, as the representative 'Lamb of God'. He did not deserve to die. In fact, the New Testament goes even further by saying he lived without sin – in other words, he showed to perfection what a human life should be. He satisfied all the demands of the old Jewish law and, unlike the rest of us, came out without a stain on his character. That's why the Cross has become the symbol of Christianity.

DID JESUS REALLY DIE?

Jesus died in unusually quick time – about six hours. The four executioners examined his body before a friend, Joseph of Arimathea, was allowed to remove it for burial. Crucifixion was not uncommon in Palestine. The Roman executioners knew their job. Jesus died on the Cross, slowly and painfully. He held conversations on the Cross, both with John his disciple and with one of the others crucified alongside him. The Roman soldiers were professionals and knew a dead man when they saw one. To hasten death they broke the legs of the dying. Jesus, they discovered, was already dead.

To make doubly sure they pierced his heart with a spear. We are told on John's eye-witness authority that blood and water came out of Jesus's side. It is known now that when the heart ruptures, the red corpuscles clot and the white corpuscles separate into a serum. What John saw was the clinical proof that Jesus had died of a ruptured heart. The blood escaped into the pericardium and separated into clot and serum: proof positive that Jesus was dead.

HIS BURIAL

Jesus is buried in Joseph of Arimathea's tomb, a rock tomb. The body would have been placed on a stone ledge, wound tightly in strips of cloth and covered with spices, about seventy-five pounds in weight. All of this makes nonsense of theories that Jesus was not really dead or that he revived, crept out and deceived the disciples into thinking he was risen. Now with any other person the story ends there, with the finality of death; but not with Jesus. As Saint Paul puts it with his customary elegance and bluntness, we have to deal with the reports of his Resurrection. 'If there is no resurrection of the dead, then not even Christ has been raised. And if Christ has not been raised, our preaching is useless and so is your faith. More than that, we are then found to be false witnesses about God, for we have testified about God that he raised Christ from the dead' (1 Cor. 15: 13–15). Without the Resurrection, Jesus died a hopeless failure.

EVIDENCE FOR THE RESURRECTION

The first point in the evidence for the Resurrection is the empty tomb. There is no body. The body was not stolen – there were guards on the tomb and in any case, there was a massive stone rolled across the front of it. Two pieces of pagan evidence come into play here. The Jewish historian Josephus Flavius wrote, 'When Pilate had condemned Jesus to the Cross, upon his impeachment by the principal men among us, those who had loved him from the first did not forsake him, for he appeared to them alive on the third day' (*Jewish Antiquities*, 18.3.3.).

The other evidence for the empty tomb is even earlier: an imperial edict belonging to the reign of either Tiberius (AD 14–37) or Claudius (AD 41–54) called the Nazareth Inscription. This is a warning of heavy penalties for any who meddle with tombs. It looks like news of the empty tomb got back to Rome – Pilate would have reported it as rifled.

Secondly, the Resurrection appearances described and recorded in Scripture are not told in a way that anyone fabricating them would have invented. If you or I wanted to write the story of a man risen from the dead, we'd make it dramatic and unmistakable, with flashes of light and bursts of thunder. The Gospels, however, speak simply of a familiar figure by the water's edge giving fishing instructions to his fishermen friends. He cooks fish and eats it. This risen Jesus has a body that is spiritual yet has substance – he eats food yet can walk through walls. Even Mary Magdalene mistakes Jesus for a gardener in the grounds of the tomb. It is his unmistakable voice calling her 'Mary' that causes her to reply 'Master'.

Again two disciples hold conversation with Jesus on the road to Emmaus without twigging who they are with. All of this has the ring of truth about it.

Thirdly, the existence of the early church itself is perhaps the most convincing evidence of all. In the words of Professor C.F.D. Moule, who was Regius Professor at Cambridge when I was a student:

> All the evidence converges on the conclusion that there was nothing to discriminate Christians initially from any other Jews of their day EXCEPT their convictions about Jesus and that it was these that kept them from lapsing back into Judaism or rather ultimately forced them out of Judaism. As an historical phenomenon the coming into existence of the church cannot be explained by anything except its distinctive features and these are due if not to a huge reality then to deliberate lying or to misapprehension

and neither of these latter circumstances seems adequately to account for the facts.*

Fourthly, the disciples were transformed. No hallucination or wish fulfilment can explain the extraordinary transformation of the disciples from frightened men into fearless proclaimers of the message that Jesus had risen.

Finally, verification comes from eye-witnesses. All Jesus's resurrection appearances are recorded and Paul even lists those to whom Jesus appeared. There were plenty of named individuals who could confirm or deny that Jesus was risen. One of these was Jesus's brother, James.

What are we left with? We are left with the most remarkable man who ever lived – one whose life was to turn the world upside down. Millions of people have found in the person of Jesus Christ someone with whom they can identify and someone who personifies the qualities and character of God himself. This is because he is God.

No one can be indifferent about the Jesus of history because he is the Jesus who is proclaimed by the Church today. If Jesus is just a good man who lived long ago, if that is all he is, he can be forgotten. If he is alive, however, and if his death and Resurrection represent the most important event in recorded history, then we are presented with a dilemma and a choice. The response Jesus demanded of those who heard him was a simple one – he demanded repentance and faith. He called on people to come to him.

To my mind the combination of historical and archaeological evidence and the testimony of Christian experience through the centuries, underpinned by my personal experience as a believing and practising Christian, means that the decision of what to make of Jesus is a relatively easy one. Journalists are renowned for their scepticism and cynicism. Historians are loath to commit themselves without examining the evidence. Theologians seek out form and literary explanations for biblical evidence. I studied History and Theology before becoming a

* C.F.D. Moule, *The Phenomenon of the New Testament*, SCM Press, 1967.

Confidence in Christian Origins

journalist. I have to tell you that I am happy to be counted amongst those who believe in the claims of Jesus Christ. I am a Christian and for me the weight of evidence is conclusive and the test of experience endorses it. Christians have no reason to fear for their faith or to worry that what they believe cannot stand up to scrutiny. Can we who are Christians be confident that what we believe will survive any amount of examination and testing? We can and it does. End of story.

8
CONFIDENCE WHERE IT COUNTS

Germany's leading golfer was about to receive the most famous Green Blazer in the world, given only to those who win the prestigious World Masters Golf Championship, played each year at Augusta in Georgia. It was his second victory in the Masters. As millions of television viewers in the United States and Europe watched Bernhard Langer waiting to receive the winner's jacket, he was asked by the American sports anchorman how he felt. 'It is always special to win the greatest tournament, especially on Easter Sunday when my Lord was resurrected,' replied Bernhard. The interviewer was taken aback. Langer was smiling. A confident Christian does not miss an opportunity to share his faith, even if, as in Langer's case, there are millions hanging on every word.

In the last few chapters we have taken a journey through those areas where we find doubt getting in the way of confidence and our own feelings often at odds with the facts. There's nothing unusual about doubt, nor is it wrong. I'd be suspicious of anyone who in their heart of hearts did not have doubts, questions and reservations from time to time. Of course, no one wants to become so preoccupied with doubt that it undermines faith. It cannot be ignored; it must be faced and worked through, but at the same time it should not be over-indulged. Doubt can be like a terrier chewing a bone. Often the dog is still chewing away long after the last vestige of meat and marrow has departed. So, too, doubt can be allowed to chew away at our faith when the cause of the doubt has been long resolved. A Christian who never asks 'Why, God?' is arguably living life at too superficial a level. But doubt is a bus stop, not a terminus.

The route you travel should be one of quiet confidence, tested by fire in daily living. Personal faith is not something to be kept in the deep-freeze to be brought out in emergencies. Faith has its own dynamic and its own momentum. It cannot be locked away for personal viewing only. It is like a spring of living water that must find a route to the surface. When I saw the source of Malvern water, the purest and finest mineral water I have ever tasted, it was gushing out of the hillside with great force. Like cricketer Ian Botham facing the fast bowling of Australian Dennis Lillee in the epic battle for the Ashes in 1981, you cannot keep a good man down. Even though the ball was flying past his ears at over ninety miles per hour, Botham swung his bat and sent the ball into orbit. If that was cricket confidence at its peak, so, too, every Christian should strive to use the opportunity that life brings to share our faith.

TRUE CONFIDENCE

I argued in the first chapter that confidence comes from within. It is not a coat you slip on when you need protection from the cold. It is not a convenient mask to hide inner anxieties and uncertainties. That isn't confidence, it is play acting and phoney. Anyone can see through it. Confidence is an openness and a sense from within that whatever happens, God is with you in the experience and you will come through it intact. The confident person is not afraid to show feelings, to express thoughts, to confide in others. The confident person can listen as well as talk. It's the deep confidence that Paul spoke of in his letter to the wayward Christians of Corinth: 'If you think you are standing firm, be careful that you don't fall! No temptation has seized you except what is common to man. And God is faithful; he will not let you be tempted beyond what you can bear. But when you are tempted, he will also provide a way out so that you can stand up under it' (1 Cor. 10: 12–13).

Confidence should become for every Christian a part of normal living. It should run through our veins like blood, a faith

Confidence Where it Counts

that is based on foundations that are secure and matured over time and experience. Like a good claret, faith should have a body and depth to it, a colour that entices and a taste that excites and lingers. Confidence is not a thin veneer on our Christian lives, it is something that springs out of our inner life. Jesus often used pictures to make a point. In one of his parables, the vehicle for much of his teaching, he compares the Christian to a tree and its fruit:

> No good tree bears bad fruit, nor does a bad tree bear good fruit. Each tree is recognised by its own fruit. People do not pick figs from thorn-bushes, or grapes from briers. The good man brings good things out of the good stored up in his heart, and the evil man brings evil things out of the evil stored up in his heart. For out of the overflow of his heart his mouth speaks. (Luke 6: 43–45)

Who we are will determine how others see us and hear us. Our lives must back up our words. If we are truly disciples and followers of Jesus, aiming to live out his standards in our lives and to show his love, then the confidence we need to do the job will come from within. When one of the Gospel writers, Luke, turned to the history of the Church and wrote his account of Christian origins in the Acts of the Apostles, he told the story of Peter and Paul before the Jewish Council, the Sanhedrin. They were arrested and jailed for preaching about the Resurrection. Before the Sanhedrin they were questioned about their healing of a paralysed man and their message. Peter, 'filled with the Holy Spirit', did not pull his punches. You can read the story for yourself in Acts 4 in the New Testament.

Peter said, 'It is by the name of Jesus Christ of Nazareth, whom you crucified but whom God raised from the dead, that this man stands before you healed' (Acts 4: 10). In case they missed the point, he affirmed just for them that 'Salvation is found in no one else, for there is no other name under heaven given to men by which we must be saved' (4: 12). Luke records the reaction of these rulers, elders and highly educated teachers of the law:

> When they saw the courage of Peter and John and realised that they were unschooled, ordinary men, they were astonished and they took note that these men had been with Jesus. But since they could see the man who had been healed standing there with them, there was nothing they could say (4: 13–14).

Told then to refrain from their teaching about Jesus, Peter and John were uncompromising. 'We cannot help speaking about what we have seen and heard' (4: 20). Later in the chapter we read of how the two men returned to the Christian community and prayed with them. Each person present was filled with God's Spirit and 'spoke the word of God boldly' (4: 31).

That is the experience of Christians who do not cringe with fear at talking about their faith, but who discover in adversity that God does provide from within, through his Spirit's agency, a courage and boldness to do the job. If we are talking about confidence where it counts, it must show itself in any situation where an opportunity arises or is created by us to be honest about what we believe and why. This task can be shared by Christians, working together within churches with a clear strategy for growth.

WORKING TOGETHER

A few years ago, 'outward bound' management courses were all the rage amongst large companies. Middle managers were being sent off to spend a night roughing it on some chilly, windswept hilltop, or were set some assignment in hostile terrain. I found myself sent on such a course, but fortunately mine was one of the gentler variety, where the toughest physical challenge was an assault course, with ropes, logs and netting connecting one tree to the next. Although each person was tied to a safety harness to prevent accidents, some of the ropes were high above the ground. The whole course was cannily designed so that no one could complete it without a great deal of help from colleagues. The leaps from one staging post to the next were always just that little bit too far to attempt without a helping hand to pull you across.

My favourite exercise took place on the tranquil waters of Lake Windermere. Our task was to take out a 'whaler' in a race across a small part of the lake. This was a large rowing boat which needs a crew of five. There was one person on the tiller, two holding the long oars and two with the short oars. I found myself in the stroke position on a short oar. After a short demonstration of technique, from how to hold the oars to how to turn the boat 180 degrees and 360 degrees, we started to row. Most of us were novices. The two boats eventually started to move as if we had some idea about what we were doing. It was then that our task was set. We were told to race across the lake to a marker buoy half a mile away. On the whistle we were off. This wasn't exactly Oxford versus Cambridge in the Boat Race on the Thames, but it felt like it. It was terrific. With one goal, to reach the buoy first, the two boats set off.

In my boat we began to syncronise our strokes, pulling together. Each member of the crew had no choice but to pull his weight. As we drew alongside our rivals in the other boat, it needed more strength, pulling deeper and harder and moving together in a rhythm. Although members of the other crew were bigger than us, we pulled together better and dug deeper into ourselves. It was hard work, but as the pressure mounted and the buoy came into sight, we focused down on the target and went for it. We began to pull away from the other boat. By working together with heart, body and mind towards one goal, we went on to win the race. It was a great feeling.

For the Christian, Jesus has already set out our marker buoy. He has launched the boat and he sits at the tiller. He wants us on board pulling at the oars with all of our physical, mental and spiritual strength. The task he has set is on one level very simple. He has set it for each of us who follow him and call ourselves Christians. It is this: 'Go and make disciples of all nations, baptising them in the name of the Father and of the Son and of the Holy Spirit, and teaching them to obey everything I have commanded you' (Matt. 28: 19). Jesus will not abandon the boat, for, as he says, 'Surely I am with you always, to the very end of the age' (28: 20).

The terms of the Great Commission are explicitly clear. I do not believe that for the Christian this is an optional extra, an activity for those who 'like that kind of thing'. It is a task to which each one of us who follows Jesus is called. The New Testament is full of alternative words for 'Christian' which, curiously, is hardly used in the New Testament. We are called to be 'witnesses' or 'fishers of men' or 'ambassadors'. Paul tells the church in Corinth that God 'has committed to us the message of reconciliation. We are therefore Christ's ambassadors, as though God were making his appeal through us' (2 Cor. 5: 19–20). We are to be 'children of light', each one called to fulfil the Great Commission. Easily said, but how do we do it?

Interestingly, if you take a long look at the book of Acts, there is a pattern that emerges of the principles of church growth, first-century-style. Staying detached from the story isn't easy, I assure you. The book is so action-packed and gripping that I'm surprised Stephen Spielberg hasn't tackled it yet. You could call it 'Close Encounters of the Spiritual Kind', or maybe 'Ecstatic Park'. The growth of the Church was based on the firm foundation of a healthy communal prayer life. Without the building blocks of prayer, and a loving commitment to each other and to their common goal, their efforts would have been hopeless.

Fired up by God's indwelling Spirit, underpinned by the prayer which is the reinforced steel of the Christian life, they changed the course of history.

On my Lake Windermere management course, we were asked the question, 'Do you believe change can be fast and lasting?' We were told that what effective managers in the United States have in common is the belief that change can be both fast and lasting. So let me pose a similar question to you. Do you believe that God can utterly transform a person's life for ever? I do. I've seen it time and time again.

Take my friend Peter. He went to Cambridge from Czechoslovakia to read Economics. He was sent there by his Government with a career in the diplomatic service or as an academic in mind. All this changed when at the end of his first year, through the influence of friends, Peter heard the Christian message and decided to become a Christian. When he returned home with his Economics degree, all the doors that should have been open to him suddenly began to close. He would not join the Communist Party and, though discreet as a Christian, he knew he was paying a price for his faith. For years he toiled away for a publisher translating Western economic books and in his spare time worked in his local church.

Come the velvet revolution of 1989, Peter's life was changed overnight. As I write this he is General Secretary of the Lutheran Church for the whole of Slovakia. Every Easter during those long years of oppression, he sent me a card saying simply 'Christ is Risen – Peter'. It was his way of reassuring me that his faith was firm, however tough it was for him at the time. He still sends me an Easter card every year, but now it no longer has Easter eggs on it but pictures of Christ or of his church. He is a man of outstanding faith and witness. For him the encounter with Christ came while he was on holiday with fellow students who were Christians. It changed his whole life. I cannot think of a more confident Christian or one who has had to pay a heavier price in earthly terms for his faith. But does he have regrets? Not a bit of it. After all, as John writes in his first epistle, quoting Jesus: 'If anyone acknowledges that Jesus is the Son of God, God lives in him and he in God' (1 John 4: 15).

Mike was an entrepreneur with a good eye for a deal. He ran a wholesale fruit and vegetable business with a retail outlet in West London. If there was a buck to be made, he knew how to do it. He bought a Rolls Royce and hired it out for weddings. He financed a friend to set up a kitchen and bathroom refitting business. He and his family enjoyed the fruits of their success and lived a millionaire's lifestyle. Yet somehow it failed to satisfy. For Mike and his wife Pat, an invitation from Christian friends to come along to a 'Carols by Candlelight' service at the local Baptist church was the beginning of a new life. Within a year they had discovered a new faith and a new direction. Though uneducated, Mike eventually felt called into the Baptist ministry and became a theological student. Today he has a powerful ministry in Warrington.

God cannot only turn our lives upside down, he gives us all the resources we need to live the new life he gives us. We may come to him with all our uncertainties and weaknesses. His forgiveness, his love and his power are more than enough to give us the confidence we need to go out and to do the job he's given us, whatever and wherever we find ourselves.

He also gives us courage and that greatly under-used resource of prayer. Praying in faith means opening ourselves to the possibility of God answering prayer in an unexpected way. It also means praying in confidence – not that God will give us what we want, but that God will answer our prayer.

I was recently introduced to an English teacher who was Anglo-Italian by birth. This lady had become a Christian at university and as she prayed for God's will in her life, felt more and more that she should return to Italy to do some kind of Christian work there. She told me how she started to pray for an Italian Christian husband, whom she assumed she would probably meet in Italy. This was a highly specific prayer – she wanted an Italian husband who was (a) a Christian and (b) would share her desire to be a missionary in Italy.

Unknown to her, the son of a Sicilian church leader came to England to polish up his English. He was praying for a bilingual wife-to-be, who could share his vision for Christian work in Italy. He even attached a condition to his prayer, asking God that such a person should live within easy reach of Cambridge where he was to study! You can guess the rest. These two people – both praying for a partner who shared a concern to serve the Italian Christians – duly met and fell in love. As I write this, they are engaged to be married and preparing to settle in Italy. God answers prayer in extraordinary ways.

THE POWER OF PROCLAMATION

What, then, are the principles on which the first Christians set about trying to fulfil Jesus's commission to go and make

Confidence Where it Counts

disciples of all nations? The first is the tried and trusted, and sadly sometimes maligned, art of proclamation or preaching. 'How can they believe in the one of whom they have not heard?' asks the eminently sensible Paul writing to the church in Rome. 'How can they hear without someone preaching to them?' (Rom. 10: 1)

If you are reading this as a believing Christian, the question I ask you is, 'Who first preached to you?' Who was the person from whom you first heard about Jesus and discovered the message of reconciliation to God through Jesus? Some Christians cannot put a time or place to their personal beginning. It may have been a gradual process aided by family or friends or school. But many can identify a person who spoke to them and then the penny dropped.

For every person the road to knowing God is personal and individual. If you get five Christians in a circle and ask each one individually how he or she became a Christian, you would receive five different replies. God does not treat us like intelligent robots. We are not ciphers in some cosmic game of Monopoly. His love for each person is individual. Our knowledge and experience of him will match our own particular needs and circumstances. The only universal factor for the Christian believer is the belief that Jesus Christ alone is the doorway to God. He is the Way, the Truth and the Life.

Many people are attracted by the Christian faith but afraid of commitment, fearful of taking such an important step. It may be for all sorts of reasons. They fear the price of letting go of their old life and of turning to Christ in repentance. They know that once they let God into their life it will change them and their priorities. Or lingering doubt as to whether or not Jesus is really risen holds them back. A friend at school found himself utterly convinced by the evidence for the Resurrection but unable to do anything about it. It is rather like being selected to play for your country's rugby team, getting kitted out but then being afraid to go on the pitch. Life cannot be observed from the sidelines. It is not a rehearsal: this is it and God wants us on the pitch in his team playing our part. Sitting on the fence is by its very nature highly uncomfortable.

Having studied the evidence and, despite my failings, having lived the Christian life by God's grace for many years now, I have to say that for me believing in Jesus Christ was not a blind leap of faith into an empty void. The Christian commitment of faith is a perfectly rational step on to a path that is well worn and well trodden. The message Christians proclaim today has not changed from that preached by the first Christians: that Jesus died, was buried, that he was raised and then appeared to the apostles and to over five hundred witnesses (see 1 Cor. 15: 3–8).

PERSUASION

Just as preaching and proclamation, whether from a pulpit or person to person, appeals to the heart, it is important to recognise that for some people the obstacles to faith will be intellectual. For them there can be no slick answers that evade the tough questions. In proclaiming and presenting the relevance of Christianity to our own time, we are not marketing a product. This is not a bag of crisps or chocolate bars we are talking about, but the power of God to change lives and to bring the alienated, lost and estranged back to him in Christ. Christians who try to reduce the gospel to slogans on a sandwich board or catch phrases on a sticker do themselves and the gospel of Christ a great disservice.

For those with intellectual questions to be answered, it is necessary to appeal to the mind. This is evangelism through persuasion. The best exponent of this in the history of the early church was, without a doubt, Paul of Tarsus. He spent three months 'arguing persuasively' in Ephesus and then for another two years had discussions on a daily basis in the lecture hall at Tyrannus (see Acts 19). Persuasion can take time, but what is known today as Christian apologetics was a central tool of the early church.

Another highly effective debater was the Christian leader called Apollos, who developed a strong personal following. In a place called Achaia, Apollos scored a big hit because he vigorously took on the best Jewish debaters of the town in public debate and won the argument, proving from Scripture that Jesus was the Christ (see Acts 18: 27–28). 'Since, then, we know what it is to fear the Lord,' Paul tells the Christians of Corinth, 'we try to persuade men' (2 Cor. 5: 11).

PERSON TO PERSON

If proclamation appeals to the heart and persuasion responds to the mind, then the most effective means of making Christian confidence count is in our personal friendships.

Family and friends would rank very highly on most people's lists of what matters most in their lives. Families can be tricky and relationships within families powerful but not always good. Friends always matter. If you think of all the time we spend nurturing our friendships, keeping old ones going, sustaining distant friendships by letter and the pleasure of making new friends, then we need no reminder of the place our friends play in our lives.

For any friendship to work at any level, there must be a degree of trust and mutual respect. I do not believe that Christians should attempt to thrust or impose our faith upon our non-Christian friends. We should respect the views of others, even if we disagree with them. None the less, it would be quite wrong of us not to share with a close friend something that means so much to us, when the appropriate opportunity arises. To be always silent on what is most important to us is to live a lie. It would be to deny a part of our life that is at the heart of who we are and what we believe.

Jesus cannot be excluded from our friendships any more than we can stop breathing the air around us. Evangelism through friendship is not a matter of technique or dogged persistence. It is a question of praying for and loving our friends so that they may see, in their own time, who Jesus is. This is the confident way of sharing our faith, but it is also the most costly in time, love, prayer and commitment. It is also how Jesus won over those who met him.

A member of the ruling Jewish council, the Pharisee called Nicodemus, came to Jesus secretly by night with a batch of questions to which he needed answers. He was a perplexed man who had a lot to lose by being seen with this new teacher. Jesus was about as popular with the Pharisees as a hedgehog with slugs. It's fair to say that Jesus did not have much time for the Pharisees as a whole. They dogged his path and obstructed his teaching at every turn. He called them 'vipers' and 'hypocrites' because their brand of religion was everything that real religion should not be. It was ruthless, intolerant and had more regulations and rules than any Inland Revenue tax return form. Yet Jesus found time to deal with Nicodemus' deep personal questions about the need to start again like a newborn baby.

Regrettably the phrase 'born again' has been adopted by the mass media and given a meaning that goes way beyond what Jesus was talking about. To Nicodemus, Jesus explained the need for a spiritual 'new birth', a conscious new beginning. This regeneration is a spiritual one, carried out by God renewing us from within. Unfortunately the phrase 'born again' has now gained all kinds of baggage that has nothing to do with Jesus's words to Nicodemus, recorded in the third chapter of John's Gospel. If you refer to someone as 'born again' in modern parlance, it implies that they are fundamentalist believers who take certain political positions to the right of Attila the Hun. All of this has next to nothing to do with the real meaning of that phrase 'born again'.

In the case of the Samaritan woman needing help fetching water by the well, within minutes of their meeting Jesus was discussing details of her personal relationships, including her sex life. He identified her need to experience the 'living water' (John 4: 10) of a deep and satisfying relationship with God, a need for love that even her five lovers had failed to satisfy. To this woman Jesus took the risk of revealing his most precious secret, that of his true identity. She knew that the Messiah was coming, and Jesus told her: 'I who speak to you am he' (4: 26). Even his nearest and dearest had not yet twigged that at this stage in Jesus's ministry, he was able to get to the heart of the matter with whoever he met. He sees into our lives and at once knows our greatest need and senses where there is pain. He offers love and forgiveness, security and the knowledge that we are accepted by God as we are. His friendship is utterly self-giving and transforms the situation.

Jesus did not repeat formulas learned in classes, or rely on memorised phrases, or fall into religious jargon. He was himself. He listened to the person who spoke to him. His answers to questions were direct, relevant and to the point. There was no mucking about. He was simply himself. And as he is our pattern and example, so in our friendships and how we conduct ourselves, we must simply be true to ourselves. We must let our trust and confidence come through in whatever way is most natural to us. When Christians learn to be less self-conscious about sharing our faith and concentrate on the business of living and being, then we'll find our friends more open to what we have to say. Our lives must match our words.

Who brought Simon Peter to Jesus? His brother Andrew did. Friends share with friends. They spend time together, doing the things they enjoy together. They share their stories and their adventures and make time for each other, whether over a meal or during an evening out together or on holiday. It matters not. Friendship takes time. Mutual respect and, ultimately, love is what holds a friendship together.

One of the most popular Christian books on this subject is Rebecca Manley Pippert's *Out of the Saltshaker*. Rebecca and I have a mutual Christian friend in the American historian and travel writer Bob Baylis. I remember Bob introducing me to Becky, as he called her, over lunch in a delightfully named pub (alas now gone) called the Contented Sole, close to London's Science Museum. Needless to say it had a superb fish restaurant. She was with her husband, journalist Wes Pippert. We got on well immediately. Here was someone who was open and outgoing in personality, looked you straight in the eye and had a sparkling sense of humour. She clearly enjoys meeting people and being with them. In her view, the reason why Christians lack confidence in sharing our faith is not that we do not have enough information, it's that we do not know how to be ourselves – warts and all – with our friends, Christian or not. In her words, 'to share the gospel we must share our life, our real person. Christ has freed us to be authentic – evangelism is not a project but our lifestyle'.

At the centre of her concept of lifestyle evangelism is the idea that we live it and don't fake it. She feels strongly that we should be careful how we use language too, keeping God-words firmly rationed.* Becky argues that God did not send a telex, or shower Bible study books from heaven, or drop a million car stickers from the sky saying 'Smile, God loves you!'. He sent a man, his Son, to communicate the message. 'His strategy has not changed. He still sends men and women to change the world. To do that we need to open our lives to others. Praying for friends is not enough – we need to share our lives with them, to let people see that we laugh and hurt and cry too.'†

HOSPITALITY STARTS AT HOME

If proclamation, persuasion and personal friendship were the pillars of early church growth, the first Christians also made strategic use of their homes. The fourth pillar was the practice of hospitality. John the Baptist spoke of himself as the one whose job it was to prepare the way for God's Messiah, Jesus. He was God's road builder, making a highway for God. The task of the preparer is to lay down the track, making a road for God down which he can travel in his own way and in his own time to the hearts of our friends. We lay the foundations through prayer. And we make the road straight and prepare the road surface by removing all the obstacles to faith that we can. If we are to take the risk of letting others see our lives, then we must be prepared to open up our homes and to share our lives.

I look back on my student days with pleasure, because I can remember all those late nights sitting up with friends into the

---

* Rebecca Manley Pippert, *Out of the Saltshaker: Evangelism as a way of life*, InterVarsity Press, 1979, p. 130ff.
† Rebecca Manley Pippert, *Evangelism (without sounding spiritual)*, Monarch, 1989, p. 14.

Confidence Where it Counts

early hours, discussing what was wrong with the world and how our generation was going to sort it all out. No doubt we had all the finest qualities of all students everywhere, we were arrogant, optimistic and full of the glorious naivety and passion of our age group. Yet in the talking there was the churning and forming of ideas and the shaping of our minds for what lay ahead. You can forge friendships through the commitment of time together, talking and sharing. Our homes provide the perfect place to do that.

I was reminded of those days rereading Paul's late night adventure described in Acts 20. Here we find Paul in an upstairs room, rabbiting on until midnight like there's no tomorrow. It was a typically hot and sticky night. A young man called Eutychus sinks into a deep sleep as Paul talks on and on. Between the lines, there is the suggestion here that once Paul got going he was hard to stop. And like all the best speakers, he failed to keep all of his listeners awake. Eutychus is sitting by the open window. The cool evening breeze is not enough to stop him falling into a deep sleep. He leans back and whoops! out he goes, falling backwards out of the window. He crashes to the ground outside. He is picked up outside – dead.

What does Paul do? In Luke's account, with the accent more on the humorous than the tragic, we find Paul throwing himself down on Eutychus, reviving the corpse with what reads like the kiss of life, then returning upstairs again for a quick bite before carrying on where he left off – till daybreak, no less! Now I'm not recommending that we try this on our home guests – raising the dead is beyond our expectations. The point is that Paul was so single-minded in his personal evangelism that he wasn't going to let a small matter like Eutychus falling out of the window interrupt his flow.

Such was the man's confidence. He was in his element, using this home as a platform to proclaim, to persuade, to teach and to share. It's important to realise that often conversations can take place at a deeper level than we are aware of. Even when we are just being ourselves in an ordinary situation, God can be at work at another level altogether. I learned this lesson in a curious way. We had invited a colleague round with his family for a meal to welcome them back to the UK after a prolonged time overseas. I can remember little of the conversation that night, apart from the fact that we got on well and had an enjoyable evening, despite the handicap that my friend had not been feeling too well when he arrived.

The following Christmas we received a card from him with a curious message at the bottom. It said somewhat mysteriously, 'I've thought of you quite a lot recently; note the card carefully.' (It was a carved oak pew end from his local church showing the stable at Bethlehem scene.) 'Am finding unexpected comfort in unexpected quarters you already know well! Not sure, but not fighting either.' It was clear he was exploring the possibilities of faith. A year later he was confirmed into the Church of England. What part we played in his journey to faith I have no idea, but to him, that evening in our home was clearly a significant staging post on his personal pilgrimage.

When we invite friends round and entertain them in a perfectly normal way, letting conversation flow naturally and being open to the possibility of talking about anything, our faith included, then who knows what can happen. If we are open to God working through us, then, as in my colleague's case, we may find that we have played an important part in their journey towards God, without us even being aware of it. But those kind of opportunities aren't going to happen if we don't spend time with our friends, just being ourselves. This may be a statement of the obvious, but it is worthwhile to remind ourselves when we find time slipping past us like a motorbike on the outside lane.

Two of the unsung heroes of early church history are the little known married couple, Priscilla and Aquila. Their names crop up just four times in the New Testament record but always in different places and always playing a key role. If Paul was the ignition for the early church engine then Priscilla and Aquila were the grease in the engine. Their home was a focal point for early church life. Luke tells us that Aquila was a Jew from Pontus and that Priscilla was his Italian wife from Rome. Paul met them in Corinth, where we discover the church met in their home. Is this the first house group in church history? Paul travelled with them to the city of Ephesus. They turn up again in Rome and receive greetings in Paul's letter to the church there.

He calls them his 'fellow-workers' and reveals without explanation how they 'risked their lives for me. Not only I but all the churches of the Gentiles are grateful to them' (Rom. 15: 3, 4). They get a mention once again when he writes to his protégé Timothy. So we find this couple in Rome, Ephesus and Corinth linked to Paul and to Timothy and using their home for God. It's an interesting feature of church life at the end of the twentieth century, that the home has become a pivotal part of church life once again. House groups, home groups and house churches have flourished. Christians have learned that the days when churchgoing was a normal social activity are long gone in this country. It is harder to attract people into churches and easier to invite them into our homes.

We can be confident that when we treat our homes as places where we can be ourselves and are open to God, then anything can happen. Using our homes in this way, whether to entertain non-Christian friends or for Christian activities, gives us confidence. People see us as we are with nothing to hide. It gives us a chance to show our faith to them in an authentic way without imposing it in an artificial way.

At my own local church we have a strategy for church growth founded on a regular and ongoing programme of activities based on the church, on community activities and on using our homes. It's a mix of church-based and home-based evangelism. In the summer months we take the church to the people by holding our evening services in July in the open air on the green outside our church. We take part in local special occasions, with floats in the carnival and inter-church services during the local Festival. We support inter-church activities like the March for Jesus and the Procession of Witness on Good Friday which brings Anglicans, Catholics and the Free churches together in a united witness.

In the autumn we hold a flower festival to bring people into the church. From year to year we change the themes and add music, arts and crafts and try to involve local schools and organisations. Our church buildings provide a meeting place all the year round for groups like Alcoholics Anonymous and Cruse counselling.

Just as we can open our homes and show hospitality to friends, so, too, the confident local church community is likely to want to find ways to encourage those in the vicinity to find reason to call in. We often forget that some people can go right through life without ever coming into a church. Their only contact at all might be a wedding or funeral. They may well think of churches as buildings rather than as people. So if we can find ways to attract people in, not necessarily just to special worship services, then it helps to break a psychological barrier. Events that bring the community together and which are non-threatening, like flower festivals, concerts, drama performances, arts and crafts displays, creative workshops for writing, dance, drama, embroidery etc., can all help. The secret is to use the talents you have within the church – your human and spiritual resources – and to use them as a platform to meet others. This builds our confidence as a community of Christians working together.

Autumn is a good time of year to hold such events. You can then build into the programme a Harvest theme and link it to a special service if you wish. You can invite those who come in the autumn to your Christmas activities a few months later, when the autumn event is still a not too distant memory.

At Christmas the services in our local church always attract large numbers, especially the traditional 'Carols by Candlelight'. When we are able to put on drama, we do so, using talent from within the church. This is very time-consuming and needs to be done well, but in our experience it is a very effective way to draw people in and to challenge them. Dreary February is brightened up by a thematic Dinner followed by home-grown Cabaret. It's what Paul called becoming 'all things to all men so that by all possible means I might save some. I do all this for the sake of the gospel, that I may share in its blessings' (1 Cor. 9: 23).

Activity alone, however, is a waste of time if we do not take up the challenge of sharing ourselves and our faith person to person as opportunities arise. Christians so easily fall into the trap of becoming so embroiled in church activities, that they lose touch with friends outside the church and fill their diaries with worthwhile but time-consuming activities that might squeeze out time for other friends.

GOING OUT IN CONFIDENCE

A famous entrepreneur, noted for her resilience and confidence in the face of setbacks, was asked about her success. 'People say to me: "I don't have the confidence to do what you've done". But you're not born with confidence. You just do it and you gain the experience, and by gaining experience you become confident. It's that way round. If you're waiting to find confidence before you begin anything, forget it.' (From a profile of Debbie Moore of Pineapple, the *Daily Telegraph*, March 26th, 1993, p. 15.)

There comes a point when the talking and the thinking come to an end and you have go out and start living in confidence. Fears have to be faced, uncertainties have to be met and you have to move out into the future. It's important not to confuse confidence with success. They are not the same thing, any more than Stilton is like Cheddar cheese. Confidence can help bring success and is a tool for change. We will not go through life without facing setbacks and disappointments. Life is not, and was never intended to be, one big 'high' all the way. After all, it is the moments of trial and stress that can in the long run prove to be the most fruitful. They help to form our 'patina', moulding and shaping our character. Coming through these periods builds up our confidence and our ability to handle later situations of stress.

Jesus was explicit on the difference between following the easy route and taking the hard and tough road. Discipleship carries a price – following him means taking up our Cross. In the Sermon on the Mount, he put it like this: 'Enter through the narrow gate. For wide is the gate and broad is the road that leads to destruction, and many enter through it. But small is the gate and narrow the road that leads to life, and only a few find it' (Matt. 7: 13–14). Knowing that the gate is narrow might seem daunting, but when we pass through it and start the Christian life, we are not alone. God gives us his Holy Spirit whose role is to go with us, guiding, directing and giving us inner power. The Spirit is that of Jesus himself and knowing this should give us tremendous confidence. We know that whatever we may encounter, Jesus himself is with us by his Spirit. We have an inner resource that will turn our wobbly hearts into a core of steel. It is a path that leads to life and that, too, is a spur and an incentive that is without equal. Our confidence rests not on ourselves, but on the same Jesus who has opened up the way ahead and now leads us forward and gives us strength for life.

PLATEAUX

If you have come this far with me, then I hope that already you not just feeling better equipped to face the future, but that you are also beginning to take control of your life. Confidence comes in surges. You will not feel confident all of the time. There will always be situations where nerves and anxiety can get in the way of effective behaviour. It's like hitting a glass ceiling or reaching a plateau on a long climb. Just when you think your life is taking on better order and shape, you find yourself facing many pressures. Your confidence seems to dip, or to hit some invisible obstacle. It may be an attack of a spiritual order, or simply a case of the nerves. It's a bit like a soufflé coming out of the oven: one minute it's a mile high and your tongue is hanging out in delicious anticipation, then it sags and your sense of wellbeing sinks with it. These are not moments for despair, but opportunities to see how far you have come.

Stress is the result of losing control. It comes with a sense of not being able to handle what seems to be piling up at your feet. Sir John Harvey-Jones, who made his name as Chairman of ICI (until 1987) before becoming a writer, management

Confidence Where it Counts

guru and television 'troubleshooter', had this to say in an interview in the *Observer* in May 1993: 'The secret is not to panic, to decide very quickly what you have to do first and get stuck in. What in your mind seemed impossible suddenly disappears before your eyes. It's something I've practised for the last 25 years'. I'm not sure it's really quite as easy as that, but he has a point.

The last thing you want to do is to sit around and mope. The Christian should get stuck in, attacking the problem on two fronts – with prayer and with action. First, we pray. Prayer releases power. Just look at how bringing God into the equation immediately changes the odds and alters the perspective. Suddenly we are not relying on ourselves but we are calling upon the Almighty God whose track record of achievement runs from Creation and the first moment of time to the very split-second in which we seek him out. That is an amazing resource at the disposal of every Christian. Secondly, we do something. Using the principles outlined in earlier chapters, we prioritise, sorting out what is urgent and important, designing a schedule and setting our objectives. Then we work out the pathway to achieving those same goals.

We must not kid ourselves into thinking it is easy. It isn't, there are no short cuts to confidence. We cannot climb Everest in a day. The journey must be carefully planned and prayed through. We need the right equipment and support groups of family and friends. We need to draw upon the resources for confidence at our disposal – managing our time and our sleep, finding space for God in a busy schedule. We set out from Base camp and slowly, meticulously make our way to the summit, knowing that there will be hazards on the way. We take it stage by stage. When we hit the plateaux, we work hard to keep going and try not to slow down. We make sure our supply route and our equipment are maintained. We remember that we cannot do it on our own.

Mountaineer Chris Bonington, in his account of the first ascent of Everest by the South West Face in his book *Everest the Hard Way* (Hodder & Stoughton, 1976), sums up the achievement and the cost, the tragic loss of climber-cameraman Mick Burke who failed to return from the summit.

Our doubts and sorrow were mixed with a feeling of satisfaction at having taken part in a successful, demanding yet very happy expedition. Inevitably there had been moments of tension and misunderstanding within the team, but these had been very few and had been quickly dispelled with frank words. Our friendship and respect for each other had been heightened rather than weakened. In our race to beat the winter winds and cold, we had climbed the mountain in thirty-three exacting, exhilarating days after arriving at Base camp. Everyone had stretched himself to the limit. Each of us had known moments of immense personal fulfilment, of self-revelation or just simple wonder at the beauty and scale of the mountain itself and the ever-expanding view to be gained from it.(p. 152)

Only a handful of people will ever know what it feels like to stand upon the summit of Everest or to walk on the surface of the moon. For US astronaut Jim Irwin, who walked on the moon in the *Apollo 15* voyage and there discovered the Genesis rock, a geological specimen older than anything ever found on the earth or moon, it was an experience that changed his life.

The ultimate effect has been to deepen and strengthen all the religious insight I ever had. It has remade my faith. I had become a skeptic about getting guidance from God, and I know that I had lost the feeling of His nearness. On the Moon the total picture of the power of God and His Son Jesus Christ became abundantly clear to me. I felt an overwhelming presence of God on the moon. I felt His spirit more closely than I have ever felt it on the earth, right there beside me – it was amazing. I didn't change my habits. I prayed at the same times that I do on earth, a brief prayer before I go to sleep and then when I wake up. But through those days there was a gradually enhanced feeling of God's nearness.*

---

* James B. Irwin, *To Rule the Night*, Hodder & Stoughton, 1973, p. 18.

How I envy Jim Irwin the opportunity to be so far removed from everyday existence and in a totally new environment, able to reflect upon his faith. By any standards, going to the moon must rank as the ultimate overseas assignment! He returned with his faith renewed and his confidence sky high. We have to climb our personal Everests and take our moon walks in the everyday, in our homes, workplaces and in our leisure where the environment for our faith may be just as hostile or alien as the moon. The challenge for us is to press on in our new confidence, our faith now built on a more solid foundation, tested and reinforced by God's own rods of steel. Now is the time for all good Christians to come to the aid of the gospel.

THE BIG PUSH: PRESSING ON

I believe that, however deeply personal our experience of God might be, and however reluctant we might feel to share it with others, keeping our faith to ourselves is not an option. This is a luxury the Church cannot afford. God calls us, not to privatise our Christian faith, but to bring it into public ownership. Confidence in who we are, in how we conduct ourselves in the workplace, knowing that what we believe is based on good evidence that stands up to scrutiny – all of this should help us to be confident where it counts. And that is wherever we happen to be with whoever we happen to be. Our spiritual life is, after all, utterly secure. Did not Jesus tell his followers: 'My sheep listen to my voice; I know them, and they follow me. I give them eternal life, and they shall never perish; no-one can snatch them out of my hand'? (John 10: 27–28)

Our response to this assurance is to stand firm in our faith and to press on to live it out. God calls us to direct action, facing up to our circumstances with a positive frame of mind. It's time for us Christians to get up off our backsides and to make our faith count in this cynical world in which we live. There are certainties, there is truth and there are God-given values to live by. Christians are not the ones running away from life's harsh realities. From the gutters of Calcutta to the homeless of Cardboard City in London and the drug addicts of Hong Kong, it is the likes of Mother Theresa, the Salvation Army and Jackie Pullinger that you will find there: Christians living out their faith showing Christ's compassion to the poor and the needy. And when faith is under fire it doesn't crumple and wither away, it grows and flourishes. Ask Roy Castle. It's not the Christians who run away.

Chuck Colson was President Nixon's right-hand man with his office next to the President when the Watergate affair broke. This was the bugging of the Democratic campaign office triggered by the President's campaign for re-election. Chuck Colson went to prison, but he also became a Christian in the aftermath of the Watergate affair. His conversion was greeted with ridicule at first. He told an audience at London's Guildhall in May 1992: 'I know the whole world laughed at my conversion. It kept the cartoonists of America clothed and fed for a month.' He didn't run away. He founded the Prison Fellowship which today has fifty thousand volunteer prison visitors. I heard him speaking in London the day before he received from the Queen the £650,000 1993 Templeton Prize for Progress in Religion.

In Chuck Colson's view, 'The answer to the ethical malaise that is infecting the West is going to be as people come to terms with the living God, come together in their congregations, their lives and witness to the kingdom of God in the midst of the decay and decadence of culture'. He shares my view that it is not the Christians who seek escape from the realities of life at the end of the twentieth century. He puts it this way: 'If you do not believe in God, what do you believe in? I have discovered in 20 years that there are no atheists. There are only people running away from God, rebelling against the moral truth that is within them'.

Christians can stand confident in the knowledge, borne out by everyday experience, that in the person, life, death and Resurrection of Jesus Christ will be found the answers to the questions of life's purpose and meaning. A confident Christian faith is one infused with a spirit that is not content just to accept life, but one that aims to master life. We are restless

Confidence Where it Counts

for truth and vibrant with a passion for living that embraces and affirms life. It is not a creed for wimps. Jesus was tough on sin but loving to the sinner. It's all too easy for Christians to get this the wrong way round and end up being soft on sin and tough on sinners!

The confident Christian aims to tackle life head-on with boldness and courage. We take on board as our personal agenda Saint Paul's advice to his young protégé Timothy. Tim was told to 'fight the good fight, holding on to faith and a good conscience' (1 Tim. 1: 18–19). With the advice came an apostolic health warning. 'Some have rejected these and so have shipwrecked their faith' (1: 19). Paul even names the guilty parties. So Christians losing their way is not a new phenomenon. But if we stand firm and hold on, we have nothing to fear.

Travelling to work each day on the London Underground, I watched amused as a tourist casually wandered down the carriage as the doors were closing. Suddenly the train jerked into action and the tourist was thrown forward and back, arms akimbo, landing on the lap of a rather surprised businessman. His *Financial Times* was crushed like a tin can under a soccer fan's Doctor Martens. The red-faced tourist struggled to his feet. 'See these,' said the much-irritated businessman pointing to the spring grips suspended from the carriage ceiling, 'these are handgrips – hold on and you'll keep your balance.' We must learn to hold on to all those things and those people that support us as Christians to keep our confidence high.

'I press on to take hold of that for which Christ Jesus took hold of me,' Paul told the church in Philippi (Phil. 3: 12). And for the Christian this prize is to share that Easter morning experience of knowing that Jesus Christ is risen not dead, empowering his followers to continue what he began. Christians are in the business of reconciliation, bringing those whose lives we touch closer to God. It demands qualities of toughness and endurance, the ability to keep going even when the going gets tough. As in the song, that's when the tough get going.

When Joshua led the people of Israel against the city of Jericho, bringing down those famous walls, his feelings afterwards are recorded in Scripture. As the grizzly old warrior looked back on his life he wanted to pass on the wisdom of a life lived for God. 'You are to hold fast to the LORD your God, as you have until now. The LORD has driven out before you great and powerful nations; to this day no-one has been able to withstand you . . . So be very careful to love the LORD your God' (Josh. 23: 8–11).

The confident Christian is not content to be one of life's passengers. There is too much to do. We get our act together and we grab life as a lion hunts a gazelle. Not for us the second best or the second rate. We are only content with the best we can be for the God who gave his own life for us. We go out and we get on with it. From now. That's the confident Christian.

RECOMMENDED READING

Here is a small selection of some of the books I found helpful in my research for this book, and which may be of use for any further reading.

CONFIDENCE AT WORK

Handy, Prof. Charles, *The Age of Unreason*, Century Hutchinson, 1989.
Mulligan, John, *The Personal Management Handbook*, Sphere, 1968.
Perry, John, *Christian Leadership*, Hodder & Stoughton, 1983.
Shea, Michael, *Influence*, Century, 1988.
Stemp, Peter, *Are You Managing?*, Allied Dunbar/Industrial Society Press, 1988.
Young, Arthur, *The Manager's Handbook*, Sphere, 1986.

CHRISTIAN ORIGINS

Anderson, J.N.D., *Christianity: the Witness of History*, Tyndale, 1969.
Ben-Dov, Meir, *In the Shadow of the Temple – the Discovery of Ancient Jerusalem*, Keter Publishing, Jerusalem, 1982.
Bruce, F.F., *The New Testament Documents*, InterVarsity Press, 1960.
Dodd, C.H., *The Apostolic Preaching and its Developments*, Hodder & Stoughton, 1963.

Green, Michael, *Runaway World*, InterVarsity Press, 1968, (reprinted as *World on the Run*).
Millard, Alan, *Treasures from Bible Times*, Lion, 1985.
Moule, C.F.D., *The Phenomenon of the New Testament*, SCM Press, 1967.

OUTGOING FAITH

Barclay, William, *God's Young Church*, Saint Andrew Press, 1970.
Bonhoeffer, Dietrich, *Letters and Papers from Prison*, Fontana, 1959.
Calver, Clive, *A Guide to Evangelism*, Marshall Morgan & Scott, 1984.
Carey, George, *The Church in the Market Place*, Kingsway, 1984.
Pippert, Rebecca Manley, *Out of the Saltshaker*, InterVarsity Press, 1980.
Pullinger, Jackie, *Crack in the Wall*, Hodder & Stoughton, 1989.
Reid, Gavin, *To Reach a Nation*, Hodder & Stoughton, 1987.
Robinson, John A.T., *The Difference in Being a Christian Today*, Fontana, 1972.
Smith, Rt. Hon. John, *Reclaiming the Ground*, Spire, 1993.
Stott, John R.W., *Men Made New*, InterVarsity Press, 1966.